DEVICE DETOX

A parent's guide to reducing device usage, preventing tantrums, and raising happier kids.

Brenna Hicks, PhD

Copyright © 2020 BRENNA HICKS
All Rights Reserved. Printed in the U.S.A.
Published by Two Penny Publishing
850 E Lime Street #266, Tarpon Springs, Florida 34688

No part of this publication may be reproduced, distributed, or transmitted in any form or by any means, including photocopying, recording, or other electronic or mechanical methods, without the prior written permission of the publisher, except in the case of brief quotations embodied in critical reviews and certain other noncommercial uses permitted by copyright law.

For permission requests and ordering information, email the publisher at: info@twopennypublishing.com

Book Cover by: Jeff Bunting

Library of Congress Control Number: 2020917095

ISBN: 978-1-950995-17-2
eBook also available

FIRST EDITION

For more information about this author or to book event appearances or media interviews, please contact the author representative at: brenna@thekidcounselor.com or www.brennahicks.com

Limit of Liability/Disclaimer of Warranty: While the publisher and author have used their best efforts in preparing this book, they made no representations or warranties with respect to the accuracy or completeness of the contents of this book and specifically disclaim any implied warranties of merchantability or fitness for a particular purpose. No warranty may be created or extended by sales representatives or written sales materials. The advice and strategies contained herein may not be suitable for your situation. You should consult with a professional where appropriate. Neither the publisher nor author shall be liable for any loss of profit or any other commercial damages, including but not limited to special, incidental, consequential, or other damage.

PRAISES FOR DEVICE DETOX

"…solution is more than just devices it's a whole system of parenting where your play therapy methods work across-the-board no matter the issues."

"Very well written and very easy to understand."

"My big takeaways from your book are that now I have a system for screen time, I also have skills and strategies from play therapy to use for every day behaviors, and I see the impact that overexposure of screen time has on all behaviors around the house."

"I can't really do an effective device detox without using the play therapy strategies - and the strategies alone will not solve my device problems."

"I just wanted to share with you that as we get farther from our detox and more time on our system it's just getting better and better. We were able to take a family short vacation for the first time in 2 and a half years because everyone is balanced and regulated."

"…a great addition to the literature."

First, and above all, to the Author and Perfecter of my faith. And to the countless parents, children, and families that give me the great honor of coming along side them as they navigate the ups and downs of life. You are why I write.

TABLE OF CONTENTS

Introduction 1

Section One: The Story
Chapter 1: The Growing Epidemic 11
Chapter 2: My Story. 23

Section Two: The Science
Chapter 3: Devices Are Changing The Brain 35
Chapter 4: Making Room For Healing. 51

Section Three: The Solution
Chapter 5: Play Therapy To The Rescue. 61
Chapter 6: Reflecting Feelings
    Emotional Connection With Your Child. 69
Chapter 7: Choice Giving
    Empowerment For Your Child 87
Chapter 8: Limit Setting
    Reducing Power Struggles With Your Child 101

Section Four: The System
Chapter 9: Putting It All Together .117
Chapter 10: Building An Incentive System. 135
Chapter 11: Discovering The Results. 157

References. 167
Acknowledgments. 169

INTRODUCTION

There is a story about a young boy and his grandfather. They share their favorite memories from their week each time that they meet together. The grandfather shares an abundance of advice and wisdom from a life well spent, a journey well-traveled. The grandson shares his unique perspective and life experience as well. One day, the inseparable pair were sitting down for breakfast at their favorite restaurant. The young boy bounced off the walls with excitement as he recounted tales of playground adventures, squirrel hunts, and the huge puddle that he rode his bike through after it rained. The grandfather just smiled and listened. It was hard to keep up with everything; a new story would start before the last one ended.

"Was I like this when I was his age?" the grandfather wondered. "Oh, how amazing it would be to know all of his thoughts and feel all of his feelings. If only I could go back to being that young again, then I could relate. I could also eat whatever I want," he thought, laughing to himself. He missed a question that the boy had asked and was now staring at the concerned face of his young companion.

"Are you alright?"

"Oh, yes. I'm sorry. I was thinking about your stories! I wish there were a way for me to be your age again; I would love to see the world through your eyes. What do you think about that? Me, being just like you! Do you think that's even possible?" he asked with a wink in his eye—what a funny thought. But the boy took on a serious expression, as if he were deep in thought. After a moment of silence, he erupted.

"I've got it! You should eat less vegetables."

It took a moment for the grandfather to understand the advice his grandson had given. Throughout the child's life, he was told he would become big and strong by eating his vegetables. In the young boy's mind, the key to regaining one's youth was simply to stop eating veggies and reverse the horrible aging process that they enact.

They both laughed together. "You are proud of that idea. As payment for your great advice, I'm paying for breakfast today." The two carried on, laughing and talking. Oh, how amazing it is to connect to the heart and mind of a child.

WELCOME

Welcome to Device Detox! I am Dr. Brenna Hicks, the founder of The Kid Counselor Center and Play Therapy Parenting. My passion lies in helping families craft the meaningful connections and care they desire. My goal is to provide you with the knowledge and tools to start on this journey. Device Detox is a powerful resource that will promote your growth as a parent and help your child blossom. It is an honor to share my professional training and personal experience with you. I have walked alongside families through my practice and I have walked alongside my husband as we raised our son. Please know that you are not alone. We are in this together! We will learn new skills, challenge ourselves, and grow through the principles and practices of Device Detox.

WHY YOU ARE HERE

No matter what brought you here, no matter what has been going on in your life, I believe that you are here for a reason. Three truths point to why we are both here. First, we are here because we want what is best for our children. We are pursuing this process because we desire for our sons and daughters to be filled with peace and joy. We don't set out each morning hoping to trigger tantrums, spark a screaming fit, or engage in arguments with our kids. We want our little ones to be happy and fulfilled in who they are and what they have. At night, we want our children to drift off to sleep, knowing that they are deeply loved and cared for. We are here because we love our kids and want what is best for them. This is one simple truth of why we are here.

The second truth is that we desire to be good parents. We have this incredibly important role as a parent, and we want to be effective in order to honor the privilege of caring for our little ones. We want to communicate with our children, instruct them, and understand their needs. Many of us have worked hard to learn how to communicate with our partners, friends, and co-workers: other adults who are in the same life stage as us. Now, we are trying to learn how to communicate with a small child; a tiny little person who cannot fully explain how they feel or what they are experiencing. As a parent, we want to understand our children's emotions and concerns. We care for our kids, and we want to be equipped, but sometimes we just don't know how to effectively relate or communicate with them.

We want what is best for our children and we want to be confident parents. Therefore, the third and final truth is that we want to grow. Thankfully, growth is always possible! No matter how hard this week, month, or past year has been—believe that we all can grow and experience more satisfying days ahead. We do not have to be stuck here. Life invites us to try and try again. A significant obstacle to growth is fear. We fear that we aren't good enough, that we will let our kids down, and be judged for how they behave in public. These are real-life fears with which every parent wrestles. These fears lead us to doubt ourselves; these fears crush our hope and confidence. Through this process, we can recognize that these fears exist and we can grow beyond them. We will learn, we will advance, and we will find greater confidence in who we are as parents.

EVERYTHING IS CONNECTED

Now that we have established our reasons for being here, I want to assure you that you have come to the right place. There is a scientific connection between behavior and overexposure to devices. Device Detox has the information you need to help reduce screen time and eliminate power struggles with your kids. I know this is possible because these two challenges are connected, and I have devised a system and found a solution for both. As a counselor and play therapist, I have had the privilege of working with many parents and children. I am passionate about connecting with families. I love what I do. Throughout my career, I have noticed a distinct pattern emerge among the families that walk through my door. Their children are distracted, distant, and disconnected from the world around them. Instructions go unheard or are blatantly ignored. Some children have become more impatient, throwing tantrums when they don't get what they want. I encountered innumerable clients who described their kids having meltdowns when told "no" or "time to put that away." I've heard parents explain that the only way to get through a meal at a restaurant or survive a shopping trip is to provide an electronic device for their children. Communication is difficult, the emotions are extreme, and there isn't a clear path to navigate through it.

As I listened to my clients voice these concerns again and again, the struggle became more apparent. I discovered that many of these behaviors centered around electronic devices and screen time. Devices are everywhere, and addiction to screen time is a growing concern for the modern family. Unfortunately, many parents do not realize the impact that these devices have on their children. It feels easy and convenient to hand a young child a device or sit them in front of the television. Maybe we need to get some work done around the house, we are trying to get ready in the morning, or we simply need a moment of peace. We, as parents, are buying time by relying on devices without fully understanding the cost.

Device overexposure is a real and tangible problem that can no longer be ignored. Children's behavior will change as a result of excessive screen time, and their brains incur damage. You have likely witnessed kids in a zombie-like state as they stare into a screen, disconnected from the environment around them. When a device is turned off or taken away, our precious sons and daughters suddenly erupt into tantrums and fits. In addition to a general lack of knowledge regarding the consequences of device use, many parents do not have the tools or skills needed to effectively dial down screen time or take on a device detox. Thankfully, this is an opportunity to tackle this issue head on and expand our ability to lead our family into better days ahead.

MY JOURNEY

I am so passionate about this subject because I've been where you are. My husband and I are proud parents of an incredible son. When he was six years old, he started demonstrating behavioral changes that concerned us. We were in the middle of one of those big life moments; we were moving. Each evening, my husband and I came home from work and needed to spend time preparing for the move. We found it helpful to put on a show or movie for our child while we packed up the house. It seemed like a win for everyone because our son enjoyed the educational content we put on and we were able to tackle time-sensitive tasks. Once moved into our new house, we needed the time each evening to unpack, so the practice of giving our son a device each night continued. After many weeks of this new routine, we began to notice the changes. Our son had grown disconnected from the world around him. He became singularly focused on what was happening on the screen in front of his face. He also grew more irritable when it was time to stop watching or take a break. My easygoing son was becoming angry and frustrated, throwing fits when confronted with instructions. These behaviors just weren't like him. Something was impacting him, and I had to figure out what it was.

I struggled to find a resource that could provide me with both information on what was happening, and advice about how to address it. Fortunately, I'm a children's therapist. I understand child development. I understand child psychology: the behaviors, emotions, and mental processes at work in the minds of children. I had the training and the tools to connect these new behaviors to one thing: screen use. Identifying the source of the problem brought some initial relief, but I still didn't have a method to help reverse the situation in a healthy manner. Merely taking away the devices and cutting out screen time was not the solution; this caused more problems!

I designed a process, tweaked things through trial and error, and ended up finding a practical solution and system that works. I wish someone could have put this book in my hands in 2016—it would have saved our family from a lot of headaches! I am genuinely thankful to be in a position to share this system with you now. This is not just about my personal experience. This book is driven by data and research coming directly from the scientific community. It is rooted in effective and reputable Play Therapy principles. I am confident that the information in this book will help anyone who is committed to implementing this system with their children.

WHERE DEVICE DETOX WILL TAKE YOU

I am sure you have questions, concerns, and doubts. I always ask parents in my practice to trust me and trust the process. That principle applies here, too. There will be times when it is hard, things won't seem possible, and you may not see how the pieces all fit together. That is okay. It's a normal part of learning and trying something new. Do not doubt your ability to grow as a parent or your child's ability to overcome device dependency. Device Detox has the principles and knowledge that you need to navigate through this struggle.

Be excited about learning something new because it will benefit both you and your child. Be enthusiastic about it, commit to it, and trust the process. By the time we finish this book, you will have a parenting system that goes far beyond just reducing the tantrums related to screens. You are going to have a greater ability to understand and communicate with your children and they will feel more secure and supported. You will be able to set effective limits and build up their self-esteem; you will be able to give them meaningful choices with the freedom to make decisions. It's all here! Whatever brought you to this book, I'm glad you are here. I encourage you to take the journey to discover more of the danger that devices bring, *The Science* behind it, and *The System* to overcome it. Don't put any pressure on yourself to have perfect results in a certain amount of time. Accept the fact that parenting is hard and device addiction is a legitimate problem. Take one step at a time and commit to the process. Enjoy the ride. Enjoy the journey. You are not alone. You have come to the right place.

SECTION ONE: THE STORY

1 THE GROWING EPIDEMIC

Welcome to the first chapter of Device Detox! This is truly an exciting moment. This chapter marks the beginning of something great for you and your family. It is an honor to share this experience with you; we are in this together. So, this is where our journey begins: we are diving into the growing epidemic of device overexposure. It's likely that you are already aware of this trend on some level. It may be your intuition, perhaps a conversation with a friend or family member. Something or someone tipped you off, or you wouldn't be here, reading this book. We cannot successfully move forward without taking an honest look at where we are now. The first step in laying out the path through Device Detox is acknowledging where we are and what brought us here.

HOW WE GOT HERE

It wasn't long ago that handheld screen devices existed only as futuristic fantasy. They were imagined in the same landscape as floating cars, robotic housemaids, and intergalactic space travel. However, in reality, many of these seemingly impossible ideas do eventually come to pass. What was once the subject of science fiction is now a regular part of life. Virtual reality, video calls, and smart devices were all displayed in movies like Back To The Future 2. When the movie came out in 1989, none of those technologies existed in private homes, let alone in the hands of children. The closest thing that we had at the time was the handheld Nintendo Game Boy, which first arrived in American homes earlier that year. Over the course of thirty years, handheld gaming systems evolved. The emergence of bigger and brighter screens, endless hours of content, and the connection of wireless internet have surpassed what most people could have dreamt of in the late 1980's.

The most significant jump in technology and access to devices happened within the past ten years. An easy way to demonstrate the shift in technology as it relates to children is to examine some of the most popular gifts given to our kids over several decades. In the 1940's, popular gifts included The Slinky, Magic 8 Ball, and Silly Putty. In the 1970's, coveted gifts included Star Wars Action Figures and The Pet Rock. Through the 1990's, children were excited to receive a Game Boy, Furby, Beanie Babies, and Super Soakers. (By the way, we are still waiting for Beanie Babies to appreciate in value the way we all thought they would). Finally, popular gifts in the 2010's have included iPads, Xbox, Kindle, and the Nintendo Wii. There is a dramatic difference between the technology our children use today and past generations. Do you remember your first cell phone? How does it compare to today's smartphones? Have you ever thought about the Christmas presents you received as a small child and how they compare to what kids are asking for today?

Our current reality was a dream to our parents and grandparents. You and I have transitioned through the emergence of this new technology, our children know it first hand. I want to assure you that children today are not worse than we were, or our parents were. Each generation faces its own challenges and struggles. The problem we face today with devices is, in part, exemplified by our children's behavior. However, it also appears in our parenting. This technology is a new reality for kids and parents alike. This is not just a kid problem with kid solutions; it is also a parenting problem with parenting solutions. A past generation had pet rocks, and they had pet rock problems. Today, our children face problems surrounding devices. They have endless access to a world of addictive games and content, streaming in high definition, and available by the touch of a finger.

> *this is not just a kid problem with kid solutions; it is also a parenting problem with parenting solutions.*

Device addiction and overexposure to screens are new problems. New problems have limited solutions and systems. One response to this growing epidemic has come in the form of health centers that have slowly opened across the country and the world. At these facilities, people are admitted, usually voluntarily, for detox of devices, technology, and electronics. These programs are for adults, teenagers, and even children. They are inpatient facilities where people go to stay for weeks, sometimes months. There have also been wilderness detox centers in which patients go out into the wilderness and are completely off the grid without electronics or technology. Perhaps you have heard of this kind of treatment. Unfortunately, the general public is not widely informed on how serious device addiction can be or what options exist to address this issue.

WE HAVE SEEN THIS HAPPEN BEFORE

Devices and screen content are new to us. As a new product, there is a massive opportunity to make money off of the technology. I believe that some of what we are seeing today mirrors what happened in the 1950's regarding tobacco use. Tobacco companies began to promote and market cigarettes as something fresh and common. It became trendy to smoke because the tobacco companies used athletes and celebrities to endorse smoking. They created unique advertisements for print, and commercials for the emerging television market. Suddenly it became very popular and desirable to smoke. Perhaps you have heard stories from family members about how doctors approved and "prescribed" smoking cigarettes.

The dangers of cigarettes were surfacing at this time. The tobacco companies were aware of the health risks before they planned out their marketing strategies . However, following World War 2, the general public seemed to be utterly unbothered by them. In time, the truth emerged, and campaigns drove to educate people of the dangers. What was once swept under the rug was now brought to the attention of the public. Sadly, it took many years before educational anti-smoking campaigns began to affect public opinion. In many parts of the country, it was not uncommon for young teenagers to take up smoking. Most smokers try their first cigarette before the age of 18 years old. In our present day, even a child can tell you that cigarettes are dangerous. We look back on these times with a better understanding; it seems obvious now that smoking is not healthy or something that a doctor should prescribe. Tragically, this evidence is revealed by the smoking related diseases that plague our country. Again, the science was available back then, but it wasn't shared with the general public.

I say all of this to make a point. In this early stage of living with handheld devices, the general public is uneducated about the negative effects that electronic device over-usage can have. I believe that, 30 years from now, we will look back on this present time and realize that we disregarded evidence about the negative effects of screen time in a similar fashion to the rise of smoking in the 1950's. We will dive into the science behind the concerns in a later chapter, but I can tell you now that there are real dangers. The physical, chemical, and biological changes caused by tobacco smoke are strikingly similar to what goes on internally when kids are in front of screens. As parents, we have a responsibility to stop the damage being done to our kids. That's one of our goals: to keep our kids safe. Screens are not safe for our kid's brain in large quantities of time. Unfortunately, most every child has one.

We live in a screen-centric society. This is a reality of modern life, and it is a real obstacle for the mission of reducing device use and screen time. Smartphones and tablets are commonplace and accessible inside millions of homes across the country. There is an unending stream of content available for children; content that appeals to their interests but also feeds their addictions. There are countless apps and games designed to keep children hooked and wanting more. And we are not slowing down. We will continue to see more and more devices with better technology and appeal. However, advancing technology does not mean we have to be slaves to our screens. Our children do not need unlimited, unmonitored access to screens. They need us to guide them and protect them as they grow.

THE FOUR S'S

Because of our society's previous issue with cigarettes, we can adjust our fateful path sooner than later. Because we are gifted with the benefit of hindsight when examining the health crises of previous generations, we can choose to adjust our path in dealing with the screen use epidemic accordingly. Now that we understand how we got here, let's talk about where we are going. This book combines stories of the past and scientific evidence from the present to create an effective system and solution that will empower you and your kids.

Device Detox will:

- prevent your kids from suffering the repercussions of excessive screen time
- help you address tantrums when your child is not allowed to use screens
- provide the system for a balanced amount of screen time in your home.

I will break this down for you as a play therapist. I'm so passionate about Play Therapy, and I know how effective it is. I understand why it works and how it works, and I want you to benefit from my expertise. In this book, we will walk through this process step by step. I've created a roadmap that has proven to be effective. The content is made up of four sections, each covering a big idea in the process and then breaking down how to intentionally and practically apply this information in your home. We call these four sections, "The Four S's."

In this first section, you are going to hear *The Story*. We have already explored part of the journey of how we got here—the ever-changing and growing world of devices. In the next chapter, I will share more of my own story. I hope it's encouraging to know that I've been here too, in the same position, as a parent. I have gone through this process, and I've seen the results.

Next, we get into *The Science*. This section will dive into the cutting-edge research that is coming out on this subject. As I said before, this is far more than a personal observation about my own child. Device Detox is supported by data from the scientific community. You may or may not be interested in the data-driven information, but understanding the science is the only way to grasp the scope of the problem, and is a crucial step on your path towards healing. Trust me, you won't want to skip over these chapters.

In the third section, we will move into *The Solution*. Here we introduce the principles of Play Therapy and lay the groundwork for handling difficult situations with your child. Each chapter in this section focuses on a pillar of Play Therapy, and teaches you how to use these principles as tools in your parenting toolbox. Limit setting, choice giving, and reflecting feelings probably don't mean much to you now, but these principles and skills will enhance your ability to relate to and communicate with your child.

Finally, we will discuss *The System*. This is where everything comes together. We will build off of the Play Therapy principles, creating opportunities for change and growth in the life of your family while finding a healthy balance of screen use. *The System* gets you to where you want to go and establishes the incentive for your child to follow your lead by earning time with devices. Your confidence will grow as you become more equipped and skilled as a parent, and the process outlined in this book will empower your child to grow and become a better decision-maker. Ultimately, *The System* will help you achieve a reduction in screen time and device use while eliminating power struggles with your child.

KEY CONSIDERATIONS

ENCOURAGEMENT AS WE MOVE FORWARD

This is a new and growing epidemic, but you do not have to be uninformed or unprepared. The Device Detox *Story, Science, Solution,* and *System* will be your guide on your journey to a healthier and happier home. I learned as I went through this process, both at my practice as a play therapist and my own role as a parent. Please take some encouragement from me as a fellow mom and as a professional. Here are four notes of encouragement as you begin your journey!

1. **We Can Lead The Way.** We are now living in the "future;" a new reality that past generations dreamt of. There aren't as many flying cars as they imagined, but we are experiencing incredible advancements in technology that are changing the world around us. We are facing new opportunities and challenges around every corner. Confronted with the emergence of devices, we can either surrender to their control in our home or we can lead and guide our children away from devices. If we choose to take steps to regulate screen time and invest in new skills to communicate with and empower our children, then we are choosing to lead change in our home. This is an empowering choice to make. Leading change

is not easy, and that is alright. We are choosing what is best for our kids, not what is the easiest thing to do. Every step we take, through *The Story, Science, Solution,* and *System,* we are leading the way for our family. We are taking on the present and the future together. Let us be mastered by nothing, so that we may love and lead well.

2. **Embrace The Beautiful Struggles Of New.** As we lead the way, we are going to learn and adopt skills that are new to us. Each section of this book is going to offer something new. Embrace the newness of everything and be patient. New things start off small, just like seeds. Old habits and old ideas are like big hairy beasts that will lash out and ward off new things. Big hairy beasts could be self-doubt, impatience, or frustration. Kids tend to react strongly to new attempts at reducing screen time, so tantrums and arguments are a real possibility—especially in the beginning. When we plant the seeds of something new, there is a period of time when we only see dirt. We need to be dedicated and patient as the seeds take root and grow. Eventually, they will bear fruit and blessings, but only after they are cared for properly. Be encouraged by the hope and promise of growth, even when the newness seems threatening or vulnerable. Stick with it, keep reading, and keep practicing. Everyone can learn something new. We can be the example of embracing new things for our children to see.

3. **Consistency Builds Confidence.** Leading the way and embracing new things will ultimately lead to confidence and competence in our skills. This does not happen immediately. There should be no expectations of becoming an instant expert. After

some time, you will have the tools and a system to help guide you to your desired outcomes. We all understand the idea of learning to play an instrument. Perhaps you experienced this first hand, or maybe your child shares a room with a sibling that is learning to play the clarinet. In these scenarios, there was an early stage of discomfort and awkwardness when you didn't want to hear the flat notes and mistakes anymore. But with continued practice, the music eventually improved. They may have achieved proficiency. The best advice for embracing something new is to build consistent habits around what you learn. Study, practice, and then perform. Practicing just once a month doesn't build momentum. Consistency is ultimately up to us. As we choose to lead our family and embrace something new, we need to also choose to be consistent. We want to be more confident in our parenting and more effective in our leadership. Consistency is a choice that you can make that will help you get where you want to go.

4. **Allow Synergy to Work for You.** You are probably familiar with the adage that "the whole is greater than the sum of its parts." I really can't stress this enough—if you work on specific pieces of this book, read only certain parts, or use these ideas in isolated moments, you will miss out on the synergy of how these all WORK TOGETHER. I mention several times in this book that everything is connected. That very idea is the hinge pin upon which this whole system functions. This book should not be considered as four separate sections about four different topics. It should be viewed in light of a collective whole. When seen and used as such, the whole is greater than the sum of its parts.

Consider these thoughts:
- Your story has led you to where you are.
- The science shows us how scary excessive screen use can be for our kids.
- Your children's problematic behavior is likely influenced by screen time.
- Your children's behavior is unquestionably influenced by your relationship with him or her.
- Play Therapy skills will add effective tools to your parenting tool belt.
- Your new skills will create a healthy, happy dynamic between you and your kids.
- A reduction in screen time will be beneficial to your entire family.
- Your new skills will assist you in reducing screen time without fights.

The bottom line is that these strategies alone will not solve the device problems in your home. You must view everything through the lens of the relationship that you have with your children. So, let's keep moving toward the use of effective skills to create a healthy relationship, as that is the starting point!

2 MY STORY

Everyone has a story; a weathered path that carried them to where they stand today. When our paths meet, we have a unique and beautiful opportunity to impact one another. The most profound impact we can make is to share our life and our story with the people who cross our path. We share the way we have traveled, the sights we've seen, the lessons we've learned, and the obstacles we have overcome. Very few people can literally walk through life together, but by sharing our story, a piece of us is given to another person. Our story can change the path of another person. Our story can encourage them to travel farther and faster than they believed that could. Our story provides information that can assist them when they encounter similar obstacles. This is why I believe it is essential to share my story.

I want you to understand the process that my husband and I went through with our son. I believe that you are here because you have encountered, or are close to confronting, the same challenges that I've faced. Hopefully, this story will be received as an encouragement and a bond between us. I'm a parent, a play therapist, and a parent trainer. When you combine all three of those components, you can see why this topic is so important to me and why I feel so passionate about sharing this with you.

DIDN'T SEE IT COMING

Our story begins like so many other stories. As I've mentioned, we have a son, and we dipped our toes into the world of devices when he was over two years old. It started with letting him use devices for educational purposes. There were, and are, lots of enticing applications that are educational and fun for kids. In the evening, we would finish up dinner, and our son would play some educational games and apps on the phone. Many of them were Montessori-based programs that focused on counting and learning the letters of the alphabet. We started him with a little bit of screen time, only with us, and only educational in nature. That sounds good in theory, but it's a slippery slope! We believed, as many parents do, that if it's an educational game and it's helping them learn, then it must be suitable for our little one. I recently read a study that said of all the two-year-olds who are using devices or screens, 75% of those children use them for educational applications. It is a prevalent and widely accepted practice. So here is the slippery slope: because we believe that toddlers are old enough to learn from a screen, we are willing to give them more. The belief that these devices help them learn opens us up to the temptation to use it too much. We may even feel excited and proud to give them such a great learning tool; it's a good feeling as a parent. The devices are helping them learn to read; helping them learn to count; helping them learn the alphabet.

We were in a comfortable routine of letting our son use screens to learn and stretch his developing mind. We limited his screen time and felt good about our system. But we were on the edge of this slippery slope, and didn't even realize it. We were setting the table for trouble, inviting an unwelcome guest, and we didn't see what was coming.

Fast forward a few years; our son was now six and a half years old. We managed to balance ourselves on a tightrope, still unaware that we were about to fall. We held a similar screen time pattern for nearly four years: only at home, only educational content, and limited amounts of time. However, our regular routines were about to be disrupted: We were moving. If you have ever moved, you know that it is an exhausting and busy season of life. Even though we were only moving about 20 minutes away, we still had to pack up the whole house, clean the old house, move, unpack, set up, and clean the new house. Life is hectic enough already, and healthy daily schedules are hard to maintain, which makes the extra effort of moving so stressful. We worked hard to keep our routine steady and devices limited for many years, and we were successful until we no longer could be. It wasn't until we were faced with a situation that required a change that we actually considered changing our parenting habits. Our move was the event that blindly triggered a fall into excessive screen time.

We quickly realized that our six-year-old son could not really help us in our moving efforts. Reality check: kids have a particular attention span and are only able to do so much when it comes to moving heavy boxes or setting up furniture. He needed something to occupy him and help him stay safe while we were shuffling things around. It was actually our son who offered us the solution by asking for his favorite games and educational activities on the phone. We thought, why not? It is something he wants, it has the appearance of being healthy and informative, and it helps solve the problem we are facing. Saying "yes" to more screen time quickly led to more requests for more devices.

"Can I watch some TV?"

"Yeah, go ahead."

"Can I play a video game?"

"Sure."

Without much notice, the screen time increased that summer. Again, if you have ever moved, then you know about the exhausting struggles. You know that our house was a mess. You probably know that we didn't instantly make trusted friends in the neighborhood, so we did not feel comfortable letting our son play outside unsupervised. And then, the most obvious reality: we were swamped. It was the perfect storm of too many things going on. A season of busyness easily distracts a parent from screen time allowances. That was exactly the scenario for us as life was hectic. Eventually, that summer and our moving adventure came to an end. The move was over, and our lives were mostly back to normal. However, we noticed a considerable change in our son.

There was a strange new urgency for screen-time. He became obsessed with screens and devices. He asked for them all the time! He would ask as soon as he woke up in the morning. It was common during grocery shopping or errand running, he would always ask for the phone. While at home, there was a persistent petition for the television to be on so he could watch something. Devices and screens were on his brain non-stop, all of the time. I'm not exaggerating when I say that my son asked us upwards of 50 times a day to watch television or use a device.

"Can I watch TV?"

"No, it's not time for TV right now."

Five minutes later: "Can I play a game on the iPad?"

"No, now is not a time for screens. You can choose to go read, or you can choose to do something else."

"…can I play something on your phone?"

Day after day, request after request. Our son was determined to get his screen-time, one way or another. He made every attempt possible just to have a little more.

Our first hope was to get back to the balancing act of screen time that had previously worked for us. We monitored his amount of device use, it would only be at home, and only educational content. The problem was that once we fell off the tightrope, we couldn't just climb back on. Something else had changed. We began to notice a huge difference in our son's behavior. He would be watching television or playing a game on the phone, and we would tell him that his time was now up. The screen remained on. He would defiantly tell us to "hold on" and that he "needed to do something important." Another five minutes would go by. We would continue to instruct him, but he continued to argue, escalating the moment. He yelled. He whined. He threw tantrums. Sometimes he would hit the couch in frustration. This was not like our son; he did not act like that before! None of this was in his personality. Our little boy was easy going, kind, and genuinely obedient. It wasn't this hard before; he wasn't this difficult. We wanted what was best for him; we wanted him to be filled with peace and joy.

It was heartbreaking to see our son act this way. Yes, partially because it was hurtful and discouraging to watch his disobedience, but mostly because he seemed so upset and frustrated. My husband and I knew something was going on, and that this was a real problem. As a therapist, all of these behaviors were red flags. On every level we saw the recurring issue and we were determined to get to the bottom of it. At this point, it was obvious that the screens and devices were at the center of the issue. Our son's behavior was so closely linked to his interaction with screens and his cravings for more of them. However, with little information and direct experience with this struggle, we weren't sure how to proceed.

DIVING INTO OUR STRUGGLE

As a parent, I wanted to find a better understanding of what my son was experiencing. I needed to understand what he was expressing through his behavior. I knew that I needed to dive into this headfirst and use the full scope of my education and training. I've learned how to be a good investigator. I continuously seek out new information and gather data that will help me better understand and serve my clients. So, as we suddenly realized our struggle and the connection with screens, I began to investigate. Was anyone else seeing and experiencing behavior like this? Was there any research on the subject of device use and childhood development? Is there any helpful information that I should know about?

As you can guess, there were shocking amounts of information revealed through my investigation. Very quickly, I saw troubling trends in data about the relationship between devices and children. The findings on the pairing were alarming. The experiences of parents dealing with similar struggles were distressing. There were even correlations between overexposure to screens and negative performance in school. Everywhere I looked I was finding harmful connections between screen use and child development or behavior. I'll never forget the feeling of disbelief discovering that this information was out there and that I didn't know about it. So, I continued to dive further into *The Science*.

As I investigated, our son continued to struggle with his behavior. We tried our best to lead and parent our son well, so we started enforcing consequences when he got out of control. He whined, yelled, and lashed out when he didn't receive a device or when he was told to turn it off. When consequences were enforced, he seemed confused. He was not confused by the consequence; he was actually confused and apologetic for his own behavior! He realized he was wrong after the moment had passed and would say that he didn't know why he acted like that. "I'm sorry I yelled. I couldn't help it. My brain just went crazy and I did it and I don't know why." Oh, my goodness. It was so disturbing to hear him say this. This really resonated with me. My son knew that his behavior changed, but couldn't explain why he was acting out in these ways. He just knew that his new expressions had consequences, yet he still couldn't control himself.

> *my son knew that his behavior changed, but couldn't explain why he was acting out in these ways.*

At this point, I was fully convinced that we were dealing with a severe issue. More and more research pointed towards it. A developing mind can be distorted by exposure to screens. Screen overexposure can create physiological damage to children's brains, changing the functions and responses of their minds. Everything I read was getting scarier and scarier. We didn't know the dangers in the beginning, or the negative impact it was having on our son. We thought we were fixing a problem, not creating a bigger, more dangerous one. It was so easy to convince ourselves that the devices were merely helpful tools, not something to worry about. Now, at this point in the story, we knew the truth. It was clear that we needed to make changes and develop a solution to address this growing problem. The health and wellness of our child depended on it.

FINDING MORE EXAMPLES

Diving into the research opened my eyes to see the dangerous impact to children that had already occurred by overexposure to screens and handheld devices. Our story is just one example of a child struggling with addiction to devices. I want to share a story from my practice as a play therapist. I had a 12-year-old client that I was working with and we had a fantastic play session. He had been more resistant in past sessions (sometimes older kids are not very excited to go to therapy). This particular week, I felt like we made a significant breakthrough. He was really communicative, open, and engaging. He demonstrated that he was in a great mood, and he seemed genuinely happy. At the end of our session, we walked out to the lobby to meet up with his parents. There was a tablet device sitting next to his parents. He immediately picked it up, got into one of his games, and started playing while I was wrapping up with his parents. I couldn't help but notice that his mood and attitude changed immediately. He ignored his parents when they tried to talk with him. They persisted and got a mouthy response when they asked him to turn the tablet off. He then started yelling and arguing with them; he was really defiant. It was one of the most explicit shifts that I'd ever encountered in real-time, shifting from one personality to the complete opposite in a split second. The only thing that changed was putting his face in front of a device.

This story, and many like it, reinforce everything that I've researched and experienced. Screens are stealing the attention and focus of our children, reducing them to little zombies that do not respond to a parent's call. When pressed, these lifeless children can swing to the other extreme as they react with anger, frustration, and even rage. I've heard story after story of families who have experienced these moments, seeing both the catatonic side and the angry side of their child. Screens are making an impact on the minds of our kids. *The Solution* starts by acknowledging the heart of the problem.

LEARNING AND GROWING

I'm guessing that some part of my story resonates with you. From my experience talking with parents, I know that this conversation can be overwhelming and frustrating. It is especially hard in the beginning as we start acknowledging that there is a problem in our home, and that devices are the cause. We are up against a real danger that is present in just about every home in our country. We are facing real struggles with our children, and most of us lack the information and skills that we need to address the situation. However, I want to encourage you that things will get better. Do not forget that no matter how hard this week, month, or past year has been – believe that we can all grow and experience more satisfying days ahead. We do not have to be stuck here.

Once I realized the dangers and problems that come with exposure to screens, I wrestled with some guilt over our story. My husband and I had allowed our son to have too much screen time; we put the devices in his hands. There can be a real temptation to beat ourselves up and feel frustrated with how we enabled device addiction, but that won't help us move forward. Do not beat yourself up. You're here now, and that's what's important. What you do next is always more important than what you have done. So, no matter what led you to this point, you're here now, and we can start making changes. That's very exciting! Please move on from the mistakes in your past. We are in a constant state of learning and growing as a parent. Everything is correctable if we commit ourselves to it. We can turn things around with a clear conscience knowing that we are doing the best we can with what we have. The best part of our story is that things did get better. We learned and grew as parents. We found a system that works and is a blessing for our family. I believe that my research, *System*, and *Solution* will be a blessing to you as well.

SECTION TWO:
THE SCIENCE

3 DEVICES ARE CHANGING THE BRAIN

Before we break into *The Solution* and *System* of Device Detox, I believe that it is essential to share some of the knowledge and research that I've compiled. If you are not convinced that screens and devices present a danger to your children, then please be open to this information as further evidence presented in this book. Being informed is the key to being successful. Through research and study, we can better understand and confront our problems. Gaining more information is like being given a compass. We can better identify where we are and, most importantly, in which direction to head. I have dedicated myself to this subject. As more stories like ours are being told, my mission has expanded. I am determined to share this vital information with as many people as possible.

I find it extremely interesting (and alarming!) that the biggest technology moguls in the world unapologetically limit screen use within their families. Adam Alter, in his book *Irresistible*, details industry executives who strictly and intentionally limit exposure to devices, both personally and for their children. Steve Jobs (Apple), Chris Anderson (Wired), Evan Williams

(Blogger, Twitter, and Medium), and Lesley Gold (analytics company) all report avoidance of technology use in their homes. This begs the question: What do those with inside knowledge of the industry understand about the dangers, addictive properties, and negative outcomes that we don't?

> *what do those with inside knowledge of the industry understand about the dangers, addictive properties, and negative outcomes that we don't?*

Unfortunately, the conversations around device addiction and overexposure to screens have primarily been restricted to the scientific community. The information and potential danger have not reached much farther than academic classrooms. By having this research and news in your hands, you are going to be among the most informed and prepared parents on this topic. I hope this is a resource that you will share with other parents as well. I believe that getting this information into the hands of more and more people will help us take significant steps as a society to address this as a real issue. Again, this information should lead and guide us to make the changes for our children and for our own parenting habits. Understanding and sharing this information will help influence our direction and approach to children's screen time.

THE BRAIN, CHEMICALS, & ADDICTION

The information in this chapter is going to focus on the scientific connection between screen-based devices and the brain. I will start by sharing a fascinating and helpful resource on this subject that is full of scientific research. Dr. Nicholas Kardaras is one of the country's leading experts on addiction. In his book, *Glow Kids*, he writes about the addictive relationship that children have with screens and devices. His research reveals that addictive behavior is a result of what is happening in their brains. There is a clear scientific connection between our behavior and the chemicals that are released in our brains. These chemicals serve different purposes. In the case of devices, there is a distinctive roadmap that leads to addictive behaviors which results from overexposure to devices. Let's get into these different hormones and chemical processes to understand how this occurs.

Adrenaline is a hormone released in the brain that boosts blood circulation, quickens breathing, and prepares your muscles for exertion. In response to stress or a threat, adrenaline prepares your body for a fight-or-flight situation. These surges of adrenaline can lead to a fight response: body ready to defend, senses on high alert, and aggressive posturing. It can lead to a flight response: running away, fearful restlessness, and escaping into one's own mind. Adrenaline is the fuel to those fires. Additionally, dopamine is a chemical released by the brain that is responsible for sending messages between brain cells. It famously plays a vital role in how we feel; specifically, how we experience pleasure or gratification. It also influences our memory, sleep, mood, and behavior. Chemicals are released to serve a purpose, and we can see that these two chemicals help us achieve preparedness and pleasure.

In Kardaras' book, the research observed adrenaline in kids while they played video games. The results: adrenaline was released while interacting with screens. That makes sense, right? There is stress to complete the level, solve the puzzle, or stay alive (depending on the video game). Adrenaline is released to heighten focus and attention towards the task of the game. It also helps to focus in on the subject on the television screen. Screen content that revolves around fighting, survival, or competition unleashes adrenaline inside of the child. This places your kid into fight mode. As they interact with the screen, they build up adrenaline and the corresponding fight response. If there are no breaks or healthy limits to the content, then they stay in fight mode for far too long, and their bodies are not able to recover from the chemical rush. There should be a healthy window for cooling down and balance. Your body needs time and space to learn how to calm down once the threat has passed. With no time or place to release their tension, children bring that fight mode into their interaction with you or a sibling.

It is also essential to observe how dopamine is released during screen time. Completing a level, unlocking a reward, winning a game, or finishing an episode are all triggers for dopamine. This dopamine rush rewards our kids for performing or watching or completing something. That burst of good feeling becomes an incentive to continue playing, listening, and competing, and this cycle continues from one burst to the next. Asking your kids to put down their device or stop looking at the screen is essentially asking them to cut off their immediate supply of dopamine. It is chemically similar to the struggle that people go through when they try to quit smoking or drinking. Whatever vice we cling to, we hold on for the little bursts of pleasure that it provides us through the chemical responses being triggered in our brains.

The power of adrenaline and dopamine together is what makes devices and screens highly addictive. The dopamine release rewards our kids for playing and watching, perpetuating their desire to remain glued to the screen. The gameplay or story often elevates their adrenaline, so they are ready to erupt through their fight response. Emotional eruptions are then triggered by a simple and sincere request from a parent to take a break and turn the device off. We are asking them to surrender their source of pleasure while they are hyped up on adrenaline, and we are then confronted by their fight-or-flight response. Our first requests go unanswered as the child escapes into himself, but they can only run away for so long. There are often pleas for "one more level" or "five more minutes." As we follow with a firmer command (or even pull the plug on the device), the switch is flipped. Now we have tantrums, fits, and tears. This is the reaction of the addicted brain.

STRESSED OUT

We have likely seen versions of this addictive and turbulent behavior. The hormones build up inside of our kids as they spend time in front of a screen, failing to take opportunities to relax and balance themselves out. This is the result of a scientific process happening inside of their minds. Unfortunately, the release of dopamine and adrenaline is not the only chemical process occurring. There is another chemical reaction going on in the brain that directly relates to devices. Our body produces and releases a stress hormone called cortisol. Cortisol is the natural byproduct of a stressful environment. Cortisol rises in your brain to help you manage your stress: more stress results in higher levels of cortisol. In the normal process of daily life, there is a healthy ebb and flow of cortisol as our stress levels rise and fall throughout the day. However, we need to remember that screens trigger high levels of adrenaline and dopamine, which, in turn, create a constant state of fight-or-flight. The natural byproduct of this environment is stress on the brain. Therefore, another result of prolonged screen time is a dangerous amount of cortisol.

Where does too much stress and cortisol lead us? It can lead to frontal cortex damage. The frontal cortex is the area of your brain that influences your ability to handle difficult situations, to have reasonable impulse control, and to make effective decisions. Research shows a relationship between frontal cortex damage and higher rates of anxiety, depression, ADHD, and other diagnoses. These are severe conditions that can be brought about or intensified by overexposure to screens. While some people look at screens to relax and avoid stress, there is a real reaction taking place that can create higher levels of stress and anxiety. We have to understand this reality and seek out answers to avoid damaging a young and developing brain.

> *their brains must repeatedly watch, respond, and interact with the stimuli in their games. it all just overloads.*

When kids spend time in front of screens, their attention declines, and their decision-making abilities diminish. They feel cognitively overloaded. Their brains must repeatedly watch, respond, and interact with the stimuli in their games. It all just overloads. The concept of sensory overload has been consistent throughout all of the studies. A child's nervous system and senses are so heightened, so easily triggered, that they really run out of control. The function and structure of our children's minds are being molded by their time and use of screens.

Imagine asking a child to sit down for seven hours. If you are a teacher or work with children in any way, you will have a great perspective on this. Kids who have been overexposed to screens will have the greatest difficulty trying to sit still, be calm, and remain quiet for long periods of time. The constant barrage of content from screen time has conditioned their brains to be so stimulated that every shiny little thing triggers their brains to move, react, and disrupt. Over the years, ADHD has become a prevalent diagnosis. The symptoms of ADHD often parallel the symptoms that are found in research on kids who are overexposed to screens.

DEVICES ARE CHANGING THE BRAIN

The previous section pointed out real reactions that are occurring inside children's brains. These chemicals and hormones are all together impacting the way children feel, think, and act. I believe this begs the question: are these chemical and hormonal responses affecting the brain itself? Well, there is another fascinating study that came out in recent years that I'd like to discuss. A large group of researchers in China took a slightly different approach to investigating this growing epidemic. They looked at grey matter and white matter inside of the brain and looked for structural changes and functional changes taking place due to screen use. In this specific study, they had a study group and a control group. The control group consisted of children who had little to no recent screen time. The study group consisted of kids who had over two hours of screen time per day. The researchers divided the kids into each group and conducted brain scans. They observed the gray matter to see if it had atrophied (shrunk or been damaged). The scans showed gray matter atrophy in red. The results were shocking. The children from the study group (which experienced overexposure to screens) had red in nearly every crevice of their brain scan. Their gray matter was shrinking and being damaged. However, the control group did not have a blip of red on their scans. What an eye-opener!

So, we now understand that screen time is damaging gray matter, and you may want to know what that means. Gray matter is responsible for impulse control. Additionally, you lose your capacity for empathy and compassion when your gray matter is compromised. There are functional changes observed in this study that showed that children with excessive screen time struggled to effectively process emotions. A child that has a difficult time processing emotions will struggle in many ways. This can affect the child's ability to make connections with other children, to listen and demonstrate empathy, and to focus on the task at hand. In addition to the emotional aspects over increased screen usage, there were also physical changes going on in the brain.

Gray matter is not the only thing that is compromised by excessive screen use. White matter is also affected. White matter in the brain is the bridge between your body and your mind. There have been additional data on children who have spent too long in front of screens without sleep or food. These children get into an extremely fragile, delicate state of mind. They enter into what's known as a catatonic state. This occurs when your body can no longer interact appropriately with the environment around you. You are awake, but unresponsive. This exemplifies the extreme side of what can happen to white matter in the brain. Most kids don't go into a catatonic state. However, there is evidence that overexposure to screens (and the unhealthy habits associated with that) result in the loss of white matter integrity.

It doesn't end there. Research shows further impact on the brain, beyond gray and white matter. An additional concern is that screens are impacting the frontal lobe. Evidence suggests that the frontal lobe of a child's brain can be changed and shaped by screen time. The frontal lobe is responsible for four things, and I think this puts everything into perspective. The frontal lobe plays a significant factor in our sense of well-being. Do we want our kids to have a general overall sense of happiness and contentment? Of course! The frontal lobe is responsible for academic success and learning. It has a connection to our potential success, job stability, and our ability to find a successful and productive career. And finally, the frontal lobe has a link to relationship skills. These four things alone warrant immediate intervention. I think everyone would agree that they value these pieces of their child's development.

It is relevant to point out that the frontal lobe continues to develop into our mid-twenties. So, the dangers of devices are not only present for preschoolers and elementary school children, but also teenagers, and young adults. As parents, we should not ignore the screen time and device habits of our older children. We need to recognize that this can be an issue that still dramatically impacts the young men and women that we are raising in our homes. No matter what age your child is today, you are helping set them up for healthier habits for the rest of their lives. The importance of the frontal lobe alone should motivate us to act and lead our family like never before. That is why this is so important. Our kids are experiencing real and powerful reactions from chemicals and hormones being released in their bodies, and their brains functionally change as a result of overexposure to screens.

THE IMPACT ON SLEEP

Thankfully, the human body has a healing process that restores and balances the brain. There are specific actions that stimulate and support healing, balance, and growth in our body. One of those actions is sleep. Specifically, restorative sleep has to do with the quality of sleep. Sleep is essential— we all need it. Children's bodies are no different. Their bodies and brains need rest. They need quality sleep. Additional studies reveal that the chemical reactions and stress caused by device use are compromising children's ability to sleep. The light emitted from most devices is one that influences our melatonin cycle and therefore our sleep cycle. It might sound crazy, but our brains do react to specific wavelengths of light. Most devices emit a "blue light" from their screens. This frequency of light has the potential to disrupt our natural rhythms and patterns of sleep. These are unwelcome distractions to the normal and healthy sleep that children need.

Between the blue light, the adrenaline, and the stress hormones – screens set our children up for an inferior quality of sleep, and their body and mind crave the rest and growth they need. A harmful habit is giving a child permission to use a device in their bed as they fall asleep. It seems normal for kids to have a television and gaming system in their rooms, or to take a handheld device to bed with them, but these are not healthy ways to prepare for a good night's rest. Devices are wreaking havoc throughout the day and then impacting their bodies' ability to heal at night. Part of the problem is that so many adults also contend with this bad habit of watching television or scrolling through social media news feeds before bed. Sleep really matters for all of us, not just our children. This may need to be a change that we, as adults, have to lead by example to show our kids that we aren't going to settle for less sleep. We are going to get the relaxation and restoration that our brains and bodies deserve!

> *devices are wreaking havoc throughout the day and then impacting their bodies' ability to heal at night.*

KEY CONSIDERATIONS

THOUGHTS BASED ON THE SCIENCE

Screen usage is negatively impacting the chemistry and emotions of our children, creating addictive behaviors and expressions. Learning about the connection screen time has with the brain and behavior was eye-opening for me. This information was all there, waiting to be found, but it was new to me. I hope this information helps you understand the potential dangers of screens and devices. This is *The Science* of what can happen when kids are exposed to too much screen time; more than what is appropriate for their age and development. We need to understand what is happening inside the minds of our kids when they engage with devices so that we can make the best decisions as we lead and love our family. The struggles and behaviors that you have experienced around screen time have a genuine connection. As you digest the information that we just covered, I want to share four additional thoughts for you to consider about *The Science* behind device addiction.

1. **This is Just a Snapshot.** First of all, I'd like to state that this chapter and the information presented comes from a much larger and deeper well of data. These were the highlights. I am an investigator by nature, and I enjoy doing the research and studying; I also have the training and tools to do it well. If you are interested, try doing some more research yourself. You can go back and check out the books, *Glow Kids*, by Dr. Nicholas Kardaras and *Irresistible*, by Adam Alter. Read through this chapter again, and if anything

about hormones, gray matter, or sleep were especially interesting or confusing, do some further research on those topics. The goal is to be well-informed and understand exactly what is taking place in your child's brain when he or she is in front of a screen.

2. **Not All Devices Are Created Equal.** I want you to understand that not all devices are created equal. What I mean by that is not all devices are equally dangerous or damaging. Think about *The Science* we walked through; the release of chemicals for stress, focus, and reward. I wonder what type of shows or movies most captivate your children. Have you ever noticed a difference between the content that plays in the background and the content that cannot be ignored for even one second? Content matters. Based on *The Science* of adrenaline and dopamine, I believe that games are more addicting than shows. Games and apps on handheld devices are created with the intent of hooking you in and keeping you playing, again and again, day after day. They are designed by experts who know how to set up the most engaging and addicting gameplay mechanics, reward systems, colors, and graphics that keep you coming back for more. The more appealing and fast-paced that games are, the more addictive it can be. When the time comes to set limits for screen time, you can use your judgment to limit all devices in the same way, or perhaps limit some more than others.

3. **Content Creators Know What They Are Doing.** Part of understanding our role in protecting our family is being aware that we are under attack. We are fighting against an industry of content and game creators that are intentionally making their

products as addictive as possible. As we learn science as a means of protection, they use science to more effectively create attraction for their users. On one hand, this is a natural part of their business strategy: they want as many users as possible to take in as much content as possible. However, our point of view is that the children we love are the targets of their business. Companies are hiring experts on developing minds to help them best capture the attention of children. The sun is a more passive opponent; it does not seek out your children to give them sunburn. The content and game industries are actively pursuing us, and our kids are the most vulnerable population. We should not take this lightly.

4. **These Are Natural Reactions.** *The Science* tells us that we are experiencing very natural and normal reactions to the stimulation of screens. It is important to point out that a child who is drawn to a screen or has an adrenaline reaction to a video game is not wrong. Attraction and reaction to devices do not prove that a child is uncontrollable, unmanageable, or naughty; it demonstrates that they are healthy and normal. A child that experiences sunburn isn't a difficult child; they are experiencing a chemical reaction to overexposure. In the same way, our children are victims of a natural response to something outside of their own bodies. Our role in this battle is to understand the potential danger, and protect our family from overexposure. We shouldn't blame our kids for something they have no control over.

MOVING FORWARD

We have covered a lot of information in this chapter. I believe that the more information you have, the better prepared you will be to lead your family and move forward. I know that some of *The Science* we covered is alarming and scary to think about. Personally, research helps me understand what is going on, so I feel more connected to what my child is feeling and thinking. It is important that we face these facts and accept what is happening around us. We will never see bold and effective change if we do not accept the reality of our current situation. Facing the facts and confronting change is not easy. However, a proper posture and attitude will go a long way in helping us move forward. Pride and fear will always get in the way of growth. Don't be too proud to face the facts and learn something new, because we all have more to learn. And do not be afraid of *The Science* and research because it might give us bad news or feedback. Accept the facts for what they are and allow them to guide you in your growth.

    I want to close with encouragement as we get ready to move on towards healing and progress. The good news is that we get to move in a new direction and lead change for our families. There is freedom and hope in learning and trying new things. There is even freedom in failure because it is an opportunity to learn and try again. The encouraging news, as we will discuss in the next chapter, is that any bad habit can be changed, and the damage that is done can be healed. We can move forward and onward to a better way of communicating with and relating to our kids. We can empower them to establish healthier limits and make appropriate choices for themselves. We can do this, no matter where we have been in the past. A better future is always something to be excited about!

4 MAKING ROOM FOR HEALING

Welcome to Chapter Four! This is a great place to remind ourselves that healing is possible. I don't have the privilege of knowing your story, at least not yet. There are ways for us to connect and have more personal interactions in the future, which I would sincerely enjoy, so I hope you pursue more channels of connection. I do know from hearing other people's stories that these days of tantrums and screaming fits can be tough and defeating. That's how we felt when we were walking through this challenge with our son. *The Science* is in, and it proves that we are wrestling with a real problem, a danger for our children. With lots of room for discouragement and frustration, I want to remind you that things can get better. What appears broken can be healed. Chaos can become peaceful. We can face the facts and move forward, and we can joyfully embrace this fact: healing is possible.

THE GREAT ESCAPE

As we begin to talk about healing and healthy habits, I want to share a story about something my husband and I saw television. We recently watched a television special that followed the stories of three individuals who were addicted to screen devices. The show followed their journey through the initial intervention and resulting recovery. The cameras followed through the entire process, covering everything, capturing the highs and lows of their journeys. By the end of the show, we witnessed the impact of their addiction and the effect of treatment. We also saw the direction their lives were headed. It was incredible to watch, especially from the perspective of my own story and research.

These three individuals went through fully immersive treatment with specialists and professionals, two at facilities. These facilities have started appearing across the country. Some are located in the southwest, secluded in the middle of desert-like areas. In contrast, some facilities are located in large, busy cities. The general population is not aware of their presence, and certainly doesn't know what addiction people are being treated for in these centers. The three individuals on the television special were each admitted to programs in various locations with unique approaches to recovery.

The individuals were put on total device deprivation; it was a true device detox. One of the three individuals on the show was a teenage girl. It's not hard to guess where her device addiction was centered. This teenage girl was addicted to her phone and social media. As part of this program, she had to leave her phone at home. She cried and cried throughout the episode about not being able to check her social media accounts, not being able to post anything, or see what people were posting. It was a complete cut off. There was a teenage boy who went out into the wilderness for three months with no electricity, so he had absolutely no screens or devices during that time. The third individual was a father and husband who did his treatment in-home with the support of a therapist and recovery expert. He was still put on the total detox like the others, so he had to sell and give away all of his video gaming equipment.

These three people dealing with addiction were invited to quit cold turkey. Addiction at their level required them to reset and learn a new way to exist without needing devices or screens. All of the devices, social media platforms, and games are created to keep you hooked. Remember when we reflected on past decades of toys and games? We played games on the Atari and Nintendo. Some of us went to an arcade and guided Pac Man across the screen to gobble up fruit and escape ghosts. None of those experiences compare to the modern video game or smartphone apps.

> *all of the devices, social media platforms, and games are created to keep you hooked.*

These treatment facilities and detoxes exist for two reasons. The first is the presence of a legitimate problem. It is the same reason why drug rehab centers exist, and why alcohol and tobacco treatment centers exist. There are addictions in life that require real options for individuals who are seeking help, and device addiction is one of them. The second reason is the hope and truth that healing is possible. The beauty of the brain and the body is that it has the ability to repair itself. The chemicals and hormones that are released during screen activities will return to healthy levels when we take a break; the nervous system will heal itself. Even the shrunken and damaged brain matter can restore itself after a time of relief. This isn't permanent damage that has taken place. Also, it is very unlikely that your child is in a position that warrants an intervention like the three individuals on the television special. The physical consequences of their screen use is likely minimal, if any at all. Realize the danger of what our future looks like without appropriate action. We need to operate with a concern and care for our children that will drive us to do what is best for them going forward.

KEY CONSIDERATIONS

MAKE ROOM FOR HEALING

Healing comes when we make room for it. In the extreme circumstances from the television special, making room for healing meant leaving your home and quitting screens for up to months at a time. It meant orchestrating this great escape from the world of addiction. While this is not the strategy or system that we will outline in this book, the principle of making room for healing is important. In the coming chapters, we are going to walk through *The Solution* and *System* of Device Detox. This will give you real, tangible principles and skills to parent through the difficulties of reducing screen time while communicating well with your child, in order to arrive at a healthier, happier home. In the meantime, we can focus on ideas that are going to be generally helpful for you as we get started. We can do a few things and make some decisions now that will help us heal and grow as we enter the upcoming chapters. So, let's talk about this idea and get into some less extreme actions that won't involve sending your child out into the desert. Here are four tips about how to make room for healing right now.

1. **Draw A Starting Line.** First, we can make room for healing by being more conscious of screen time and device use. Before we discuss how to reduce screen time effectively, it would be helpful to take stock of how much screen time your child currently takes in. You likely have some idea where you stand. Do your best to precisely evaluate how much time is spent on a device or in front of a screen. Device Detox will take you on a journey, and it is helpful to know where you are now and draw a starting line. There will come the point when you are working *The System* and *The Solution* and you will look back and see how far you've come. So, find the accurate number of minutes and hours of screen time and write it down in a place where it won't get lost. You can be specific about how much time is spent on particular devices.

    Be honest. If your child is getting hours of screen time each day, then face the facts, and let that be your starting line. You will appreciate your honesty later on. By doing this, you are preparing yourself for what is coming next. You are making room for healing and growth. To make helpful, intentional steps towards progress, you must know where you're starting.

2. **Avoid Additional Screen Time.** I don't expect you to immediately take away all of the devices and screens in your home. Even for the idea of drawing a starting line, there isn't any pressure to actively reduce screen time yet. Just take inventory of what your normal, daily usage looks like in your home. However, a practical and helpful way to make room for healing and growth is to avoid adding more screen time. This may seem obvious, but it is worth stating just the same. The temptations and busyness of life will still

exist every time you put this book down. The tantrums and constant requests may still persist. I hope that the information and stories that we have covered so far will inspire you to resist adding more time to what is currently normal in your home. Make room for healing and change by not allowing additional time with devices.

3. **Be A Model.** I know that many of you were afraid that this would come up eventually. Yes, you need to be mindful of your own screen time, and so do I. There are many reasons to ignore this idea. As adults, we have the freedom and authority to set our own schedules and habits. We typically have productive things to do on our devices: send messages, check emails, pay bills, read the news, do some work, etc. We also do not face the same level of danger to overexposure that our children do. Our brains are less susceptible to damage because our brains are already fully developed. So, why does our screen time matter?

   We set the tone and example for our families. We may not realize it, but our actions speak volumes to our children. We can make room for healing and growth by modeling it. We do not need to sell all of our technology or vanish into the wilderness. We just need to be mindful of our own habits with devices, at least in front of the kids. The truth is that many adults struggle with regulating their own screen time. We don't need to check emails at the dinner table. We don't need to have our phones out or television on the whole time we are home with our kids. For most of us, the majority of our screen time is not spent doing something productive. If we can establish some limits for ourselves, then we can better learn how to establish limits for our children. We can make room for our whole family to grow by being a model for our child to emulate.

4. **Take Advantage Of Healthy Habits.** Everything is connected. Harmful habits like too much screen time can have a negative impact on our child's mood, sleep, energy, behavior, and so on. The opposite is true of healthy habits. As we prepare to dive into the next stage of Device Detox, we should consider the regular healthy habits that we can take advantage of to benefit our children. One great example is exercise. Where devices can build up high levels of stress, physical exercise can help reduce stress and cortisol levels in the brain. Help your family make it a habit to find some form of physical activity each day. You can do some of your own research into the benefits of exercise and find lots of great ideas for indoor and outdoor activities for all ages.

    Another beneficial habit is establishing a healthy bedtime. Sleep is so important for our little one's physical growth and development, as well as emotional and mental health. If you do not already have an optimal bedtime pattern, please consider this a great opportunity to schedule a healthy habit. This will create more room for healing and growth in the life of your child. There are lots of healthy habits that you can take advantage of that will help boost the potential for you to meet your goals for your family. Everything is connected, which means that these habits and opportunities will reinforce and support your journey through Device Detox.

READY FOR ACTION

The work we do to make room for growth will not be wasted. When working in a yard, removing weeds and dead plants is vital to the health and growth of your garden. We must clear room for new seeds to be sown and young plants to bear fruit. These are great and tangible steps that can lead your family towards the next season of life for your children. Make room for encouragement, for rest, and for your health. You need to be ready for action.

    We are about to transition to the next section, which means we are getting into *The System* and *Solution* of Device Detox. We have covered a lot of information so far in this book. These chapters have set up an understanding of what is coming next. Be excited! We will continue to learn new things and start the process of putting principles into action. Be encouraged because it will benefit your child and it will benefit you. Be committed to it, and trust the process. You will be able to set effective limits and build up their self-esteem. You will be able to offer them meaningful choices with the freedom to make decisions. You can do this!

SECTION THREE: THE SOLUTION

5 PLAY THERAPY TO THE RESCUE

We have reached an exciting point in our journey where we begin to uncover *The Solution*. Thank you for coming this far! You have heard my *Story* and *The Science* behind Device Detox. Our problem is well defined. As a parent, we want what is best for our children but too often we have to struggle through tantrums, whining, and tears unless we offer screen-time; we would like to offer something better. *The Solution* will outline the tools that will help you get to where you want to go. We hope to have a healthy detox. We want to reduce electronics exposure to a healthy, predetermined amount, and enforce it moving forward. We also want to rid ourselves of our dependence on devices as a "fix-all" in our parenting toolbox. We want both of these things to happen consistently without meltdowns and tears from anyone. Do we want too much? No! Is all of that even possible? Yes! This is where our *Solution* comes into play.

The Solution is based on Play Therapy. I am a Registered Play Therapist with my own private practice. I work with children and I train parents with Play Therapy-based principles, which combine education and psychology. I understand the significance of development and age-appropriate concerns, primarily working with children from two through fourteen years old. I developed the Device Detox *Solution* using my training, education, and personal experience. I have tried it, tweaked it, and perfected it. I restate all of this to encourage you that these are tested tools and proven skills. Play Therapy is the key that unlocks *The Solution* to our problems. Let's take a look at what Play Therapy is about, as it opens the door to a better path for your family.

A SOLUTION BASED IN PLAY THERAPY

Play Therapy is a principled approach to interacting with kids and intentionally meets the needs of children by using their requirements, thoughts, and feelings as the basis for how we interact with each individual child. This is a new skill set and mentality for most parents because adults often default to their own experiences and feelings while caring for their kids. Play therapy is designed to engage children in the most respectful and considerate way. This means shifting away from our own understanding and moving towards the emotional and developmental needs of our children. Kids are often treated as lesser humans because they're young. They can be disregarded, ignored, and pushed aside. Children have feelings and thoughts. We need to treasure that truth and openly embrace them. Play Therapy is about acknowledging the feelings and needs of a child above our own. We ought to pursue understanding them as we desire to be understood by them. This respect and consideration is the foundation for Play Therapy parenting. What a beautiful thing—to embrace the heart and mind of a child.

Kids work from an emotional center; everything about them is emotionally driven. They react in the moment, governed by their feelings. This is why we need to shift our approach to better match them. When we interrogate them with questions and make them explain something that they did, we often don't get direct or fully developed answers. They don't know why they yelled, hit, or cried. Our adult mind is looking for a well-reasoned response, but we need to shift to meet their emotional level. Play Therapy allows them to sit in their own emotions and not pull them through a curriculum of mental exercises. What everyone is looking for in this situation is understanding. As parents, we need to shift from trying to understand their thoughts and reasoning to understanding their emotions and feelings. This will empower our kids to feel heard and validated, which is so important.

There are four pillars of Play Therapy; each is its own unique principle and skill. They work in concert

> *our solution is comprised of reflecting feelings, limit setting, and choice giving.*

with one another. The more pillars that are used, the stronger the structure. Growing in one skill will create more room for growth in another; they are not meant to be singled out. Keep that in mind as we begin to journey through each of the principles in the coming chapters. This book will focus on three of the four pillars of Play Therapy to form our *Solution* for Device Detox. Our *Solution* is comprised of reflecting feelings, limit setting, and choice giving. These three pillars are principles and skills that will lay a foundation for success in the pursuit of effectively reducing screen time and eliminating power struggles. We will learn and practice all three of these skills. Perhaps one will come more naturally to you and others will seem more difficult, but, again, they are all essential to our *Solution* and they build off of each other. We will unpack these three Play Therapy pillars in the next three chapters.

THE HISTORY OF PLAY THERAPY

Now that we have introduced the basic concept of Play Therapy, let's take a moment to talk about where it comes from. If you have not heard of it before, then you might assume that it is a brand new method of therapy. The truth is, Play Therapy has been around for more than 100 years! The earliest documented case of Play Therapy was in 1905 by Dr. Sigmund Freud. He was not a play therapist, but he used some of the early principles of Play Therapy to help a father work with his five-year-old son. So, Play Therapy has been around for a long time, but it has mostly been stuck in the world of academia.

There are many universities that train in Play Therapy. There are even universities that have Play Therapy centers. We can find professors, researchers, and clinicians that publish Play Therapy literature. We have clinical articles that are published regularly that relate to Play Therapy and the work of Play Therapy in the psychology and therapeutic communities. Unfortunately, Play Therapy has not really made its way into the hands of the general population. Because of this, we have a lot of parents and caregivers that have never heard of it or don't know any practical way to use Play Therapy skills. We have plenty of support and training for students and therapists, but not a lot of resources for parents or caregivers. So here I am, evangelizing Play Therapy to parents on a grand scale because I know that these skills can bring incredible change in your life at home.

WHAT PLAY THERAPY DOES

Now that we have learned more about Play Therapy and where it comes from, let's talk about what Play Therapy does when we use it. Play Therapy changes the parent-child relationship. It makes the relationship better and whole. The doors open for greater respect, communication, kindness, and care. As you meet your child in their reality, which is play and emotional experience, you will better understand who they are. One day, your kids are going to develop and grow to be more like you, and then you can have great long conversations about what they think and how they thoughtfully process the world. But, you don't have to wait until your children are grown to understand and relate with them. You can learn and discover their world as they experience it now. Doing this builds mutual trust within your relationship. It produces confidence in each parent to better communicate and relate to each of their children. Play Therapy gives us the tools to make better connections because it is driven by their needs and feelings, not ours.

Play Therapy also helps alleviate the power struggles that can occur between parent and child. Children do not really have any power or choice in where they go, when they go, or how they go. We make so many decisions for them. When we say "no" or "go," and they resist and struggle, it creates a battle of

the arguments, the back and forth, the desperation—they do not have to be your family soundtrack any longer.

wills based on a desire for control. The arguments, the back and forth, the desperation—they do not have to be your family soundtrack any longer. Play Therapy provides tools to address power struggles and empowers the child to make appropriate choices for themselves. The eventual outcome is that they become more independent and even accept consequences easily. The choices then become their own, and so do the results. I know that many of us dislike having to punish and discipline, but Play Therapy provides tools to enforce the choices that our children make, rather than dictate the outcomes. We get to benefit from watching our child learn and grow through choice giving and limit setting.

Play Therapy is a unique, meaningful way of understanding and communicating. Play Therapy has been validated and found to be effective with almost every population, and with virtually every age group. In fact, our focus here is Play Therapy for kids, but Play Therapy has also been useful in the geriatric population. These skills have also shown to be beneficial across languages, ethnicities, and time periods. For your child, it is encouraging and empowering to feel understood and cared for. In fact, kids are shocked when mom or dad begins using Play Therapy at home. It tells me that parents are taking the shift seriously, and clearly their kids are noticing. It also tells me that children aren't being treated like that in many other places, which hopefully will begin to change. Children feel the difference, and they do appreciate Play Therapy principles when they are applied. Remember: everything is connected, and the relationship is at the center of your success!

LEARNING THE MOVES

This is a developed and proven framework that will strengthen your ability to parent and lead your family. As we begin to learn and train together, let's remember that adopting new steps and skills is rarely easy to do. Have you ever learned a choreographed dance or a new fitness routine? I know from experience that it is a challenging situation. I will never forget walking into my first group workout class at a local gym. Everyone was already set up and ready as the instructor began. Unfortunately, I was not familiar with the choreographed moves that the instructor called out. Not only were the moves unfamiliar, some of them didn't feel natural to me. I generally do not move that way, so my body felt rigid and stiff while attempting the routine. The instructor was so confident about the moves, calling them out to the beat of the music.

"Grapevine to the right. Repeat! Starburst to the left. Come on, do it again!"

"Starburst? What does that even mean?" I wondered to myself.

Everyone spins in syncopated steps. The instructor and the music propel the class forward, inviting new steps, and providing the rhythm. Everyone is in concert with one another. Well, almost everyone. It's easy to decipher the new members apart from the veterans. The seasoned attendees instantly and effortlessly reacted to the instructor's words. They couldn't help but chuckle when the new people slid the wrong direction, or spun at the wrong time. I'm sure I would laugh a little, watching myself and my best attempts to keep up, too.

It can be frustrating to be new, unfamiliar with the steps, and out of sync with the rhythm. I remember feeling a little inadequate and disappointed in myself. The biggest temptation to quit is often right at the beginning, because *The Solution* can feel out of reach. So, my goal moving forward is for you to feel confident about our *Solution* and the steps involved in it. I believe you can do this, and you may be a natural at all of the steps. If you're not, do not allow yourself to quit or feel inadequate as we start. Most people will feel lost and rigid early on. The steps will be new, but you can master them. The main difference between the confident experts in that aerobics class and myself was experience, not ability or desire. Over time, I learned the steps and found the rhythm. I could "starburst" with the best of them. The same will be true of you as you invest in *The Solution* of Device Detox.

You will begin to learn the Play Therapy moves through the next three chapters. Each chapter is dedicated to one Play Therapy principle. We will learn about the role and purpose of each principle and practice utilizing the skill with common scenarios. Each new skill is important and deserves its own time to learn and practice. You will become effective and confident in your ability to use all three skills and the benefits will be clear.

One final note—I know that you are reading this book because you want a solution for too much screen use in your home. So far, we have covered a lot of information, but nothing has given you a solution. This is intentional! Everything is connected, and everything begins with your relationship. We are going to look at three Play Therapy skills, one at a time, so that you have the foundation for a healthy and happy dynamic regarding your parenting. If you don't get these down, *The System* falls apart. Take the time to digest and practice each skill, and then you will be ready to use those skills for your screen reduction plan. Everything is connected!

6 REFLECTING FEELINGS

INTRODUCTION TO REFLECTING FEELINGS

We are revealing the first Play Therapy skill, which is called reflecting feelings. While all of the skills are necessary and important, I feel this is the most important skill that we will learn. It serves as the foundation upon which all of Play Therapy is built. With this skill, you and your child will develop a better emotional vocabulary. This will help everyone more effectively communicate their feelings and understand how the other person is feeling. Communication and understanding are critical to healthy parenting, and for achieving a device detox. I place this skill first.

All people have a deep need to be understood. When we feel something, good or bad, we want to be heard, understood, and validated. This is just as true for children as it is for adults. Play Therapy honors and upholds this need by using the reflecting feelings skill. The intention of this skill is to help the child hear the emotion that they are expressing. Children have not yet developed a robust emotional intelligence or an emotional vocabulary.

Essentially, they struggle to identify and communicate how they feel, so we guide them in identifying their emotions. When we use the reflecting feelings skill, we are using their cues to determine the emotions that they are experiencing, and then telling them what emotion we see them expressing.

This all begins by paying attention to the verbal and non-verbal cues of our kids. We are trying to identify and acknowledge their feelings, which takes intentional and focused effort on our part. If we are on our phone, or if we are too distracted, we will have a hard time picking up on their cues. If we do this well, we will open the door for meaningful and healthy communication. So, reflecting feelings simply starts by watching and listening to our kids. As we see and hear their expressions, we will be able to put the pieces together in order to identify their feelings. This is an ability that you will practice and develop. When you know the emotions being expressed, you can determine where that feeling is coming from; we call this the qualifier. It's helpful to see the explanation, or qualifier, behind the expression so that you both can understand where the feeling is rooted. When they know the qualifier, they can communicate their feelings from similar situations in the future. That is an introduction of the principle of reflecting feelings. Now, let's get into the framework for using this skill.

> *all people have a deep need to be understood. when we feel something, good or bad, we want to be heard, understood, and validated.*

THE REFLECTING FEELINGS FRAMEWORK

<you> + <feeling> + <qualifier>

To begin using the reflecting feelings skill, you must know the framework. The framework provides a specific and intentional way to use this skill correctly and consistently. First, start with the pronoun "you" when reflecting feelings. This is a critical aspect of the skill and it is essential to the framework. There is research based evidence to back this. Starting with the word "you" is a vital piece of communication that shows the child that our full attention is on them. Our goal is to acknowledge and relate to our kids. Starting with "you" instead of "I" communicates our intent and achieves our goal. This is the framework of a foundational principle in Play Therapy. You can plan on getting cozy and familiar with "you," as we will be starting all of our Play Therapy communication this way.

After "you," the second piece of the framework is the feeling word (emotion). This word represents the feeling that our child is expressing, both verbally and non-verbally. Care and attention is required to observe the expressions of the child and then determine the appropriate feeling word. By doing this, we establish a connection and understanding with our kids. They are seeking to be heard and understood. Connecting their expressions to a feeling will do just that. It is critically important that we start with "you" and then share the feeling word.

Now we can incorporate the third and final piece of the framework, which is the qualifier, or the explanation of the feeling. This element is a short and concise validation of the feeling. Our kids are expressing an emotion for a reason, and this allows us to show that we not only understand their emotion, but we understand why they are feeling this way. There is often a temptation to downplay the cause of the expression, especially if it is negative. Instead, the framework of reflecting feelings encourages us to be more understanding and empathetic. This creates a bond and appreciation between the parent and child. So, we put all three pieces together to make a short, concise, and very meaningful sentence: "<you> + <feeling> + <qualifier>." This framework is the key to using the reflecting feelings skill. As we prepare to begin our practice in using the skill and framework, let's discuss four tips to help us do this well.

KEY CONSIDERATIONS

FOUR TIPS FOR REFLECTING FEELINGS

1. **Look For Non-Verbal Expressions.** When using the reflecting feelings skill, we always start with "you" and then add the feeling word that our kids are expressing. Our first tip is a reminder that some expressions are verbal, but there are also a variety of non-verbal expressions and representations. Non-verbal communication is occurring all the time, and we should expect a lot of our reflecting feelings to be informed by body language, not just spoken language. Facial expressions, posture, gestures, eye contact, hiding, restlessness, irritability, and hitting are all examples of non-verbal communication. It often isn't until children reach twelve or thirteen years old that they make significant progress in verbally communicating their feelings. So, we need to have our radars on and be tuned in to these non-verbal methods of communication. When non-verbal communication occurs, we can assess the feeling, and reflect it back to our child.

An excellent tool to identify the emotion behind the non-verbal communication is eye contact. Look into your child's eyes before you decide what feeling you'd like to reflect to them. There are great country songs and love songs written that declare "eyes are the window to the soul." This is especially true with kids. You will get a great sense of how they feel by looking into their eyes. Eye contact is crucial because sometimes their behavior and their words can be misleading. Their eyes can paint a different picture than their words or actions. Have you ever been around someone who giggles when they are nervous? Maybe that's something you do. Well, this is an example of an expression that doesn't quite match the feeling. While we observe those giggles, the eyes will signal nervousness, anxiety, or fear. Some behavior looks like anger, but the eyes will show a deep sadness. When it comes to non-verbal cues, eye contact is a tremendous tool. Every person has unique non-verbal cues. We get the pleasure of discovering those particular and personal attributes, and then recognizing them as we reflect feelings.

> *you will get a great sense of how they feel by looking into their eyes.*

2. **Share Age-Appropriate Reflections.** The second tip is to be mindful of your child's age and development. The feeling word we choose needs to be within their comprehension so that they can feel understood and validated. If you are a wordsmith, you may need to resist the urge to tell your four-year-old, "You are exasperated by your baby brother." You could be right on the money, but your child could be uncertain about the vocabulary bomb that

you just dropped on them. Be age-appropriate and attuned to the development of your child. Being age-appropriate achieves an effective level of mutual understanding that continues throughout their growth and development. The vocabulary will (and should) grow with the kids.

At the same time, make sure that your feeling words are not too limited or basic. Be careful not to overuse the same two or three words to reflect the full spectrum of your child's emotions. As your child gets older, or if they are already grown, you should seek out ways to grow their emotional vocabulary; maybe you will use a word like "exasperate" one day! At any stage, if your list of words is too narrow or too broad for the age and development of your child, it will not be as useful or effective in the reflecting feelings process. There are certain words that are popular. This doesn't make them bad words to use, but they can be categorically overused in describing how a child feels. Many people tend to stick to the standard "happy," "sad," "mad," and "scared" as their only four feeling words. We can use these words when they are most appropriate, but we can also dig deeper and find something more specific and relatable to what our kids are feeling.

There are so many rich and appropriate emotions beyond the four words: happy, sad, mad, and scared. You don't have to watch the National Spelling Bee to find them! But it does take some intentional time and effort. The beautiful thing is that kids will usually have feedback when we practice reflecting feelings, typically an affirmation or correction. The affirmation is so sweet and special. You can see it on their faces when they realize that they are being heard and understood. Being corrected is not a bad thing, either.

They are going to appreciate your interaction and intention. If your word is not quite age-appropriate enough, they may let you know by asking what that word means. They may also have a word in mind. You might say, "You are feeling frustrated," and they could correct us by saying, "No, I am mad." This is not a problem. Our response is simply, "Oh, you are mad." Now you are having this small, emotional dialogue with a child and they are effectively telling an adult how they feel. That is a huge win!

As you are getting started, do not feel bad about using those four standard words to describe emotion. Dr. Paul Ekman is an expert and researcher in the field of emotional expression. He determined that six universal emotions are expressed across all cultures and demographics; anger, disgust, fear, happiness, sadness, and surprise. Again, it is not wrong to operate with the four words I mentioned earlier or the six words from Dr. Ekman. My challenge to you is to begin with an age-appropriate standard and then seek to grow the emotional vocabulary. As time goes on, do not rely on the default terms. Grow yourself and grow your child. You will both learn and become more comfortable using your emotional vocabulary.

Observe the expressions, consider the age-appropriate options, and then deliver the feeling word inside of the framework. This process is similar to completing a crossword puzzle. Your child gives the clues through their expressions, their age and development give you the size and scope of the word, and then you are tasked to find the word that best fits. The same four or six words will not fit in every spot; more words will be needed as you continue the process.

3. **Keep It Short.** The third tip is to keep it short. Remember the framework, "<you> + <feeling> + <qualifier>." Earlier, we mentioned that we are creating a short, concise, and significant sentence. A good rule of thumb is to limit your reflection to around ten words or less. Let me explain why. When we talk too much, we tend to overthink it. Instead of reflecting the feeling, there is a tendency to reflect our own thoughts and feelings as we try to rationalize about the situation. The point is identifying the feeling we see expressed in the child; we don't need to say anything more than that. We laid out a three part framework: starting with the "you" pronoun, adding the feeling word, and ending with a short qualifier to that feeling. An example: "You are frustrated that Bobby took your car." The "you" and the feeling are always going to be short if we stick to that script; the explanation piece is where we tend to overthink and overstate. Be short and concise with your explanation.

As a caring parent, there is a temptation to overstate the explanation. There is also a temptation to fix the feeling immediately. This is especially true for negative emotions. Your child is frustrated that a friend took their toy. In this moment, you do not need to fix their feeling by saying, "You are frustrated that Bobby took your car, but that is alright. Don't be upset, you will get it back later, and there are more cars to play with." Our rush to fix their feeling does not help them learn or grow from this moment. It does not truly acknowledge their emotional needs either; it actually dismisses them. If we respond to their feeling by running to give them a new toy or by taking their toy back from Bobby, we aren't addressing their feeling. We are really just trying to make it stop.

Our rush to provide a solution to their feeling creates the sense that their feeling is actually the problem that needs to be solved.

The key is to keep it short and let their emotions be heard and understood in a meaningful way. Just to clarify, we are talking about emotional feelings. If your child is hungry, you should feed them. They should not sit in that feeling. An emotional feeling can sit for a moment. It can be felt and processed. So, don't be afraid to keep your response short. Let the child and their feeling be the focus—not your explanation or rationalization. As you begin to practice reflecting feelings, count your words and see where you land. If you are hitting twenty words or more, then try again. Work your way down to ten words or less. This will help your effectiveness and clarity when using the reflecting feeling skills.

4. **Tone & Facial Expression Matter.** The fourth and final tip is focusing on your expressions and non-verbal cues. You always want your tone of voice and your facial expression to match the feeling that you are reflecting. So, if the child is expressing a negative emotion, you want the tone of your voice to be lower, calmer, and empathetic. If the child is showing a positive emotion, then you want the tone of your voice to be elevated, emphatic, and excited. Be mindful not to reflect a negative feeling with a positive tone or a positive feeling with a negative tone. It will not feel sincere. Even if you accurately identify their feeling and the explanation behind it, the wrong tone will rob the genuine connection and bond that you are trying to create. Furthermore, your facial expression should reflect the emotion of your child (on a reduced level). For negative feelings, it is appropriate to have a flat or somber expression. You do

not need to match their angry emotion with an angry face; we are just being mindful to avoid the discord of reflecting an angry feeling with a smile. On the positive end, it is helpful if you can match your facial expression to their emotions of joy, excitement, or pride. Kids are very in tune with tone, and they can read your face better than you think.

LET'S PRACTICE REFLECTING FEELINGS

Now that we have learned the framework and covered four helpful tips, it is time to begin practicing the reflecting feelings skill. We are going to use common scenarios as practice, and we are going to give you space to write out your reflecting feelings response using the framework. After you have written out your own response, we can compare notes as I share my response and a few thoughts behind it. Practice is important and we all need it. It will be helpful to use these practice scenarios with your own child in mind as the subject. This will help you practice being age-appropriate and personal. Let's work through these four scenarios. Take your time and write out your response using the lines below each scenario. Again, use the framework "<you> + <feeling> + <qualifier>" for each scenario.

<you> + <feeling> + <qualifier>

Scenario #1

In the first scenario, your child successfully climbs to the top of the playground. They look at you and exclaim, "I did it". Take a moment, use the framework, and write out the reflecting feeling response:

<you> _____
<feeling word> _____
<qualifier> _____
<put it all together> _____

Now that you have your sentence, I would like to share my reflecting feelings response to help guide and reinforce the practice. My immediate reaction to this scenario is, "You are proud that you did it." I could easily imagine the feeling of excitement as well: "You are excited that you made it to the top!" These are two different feelings, and there are other possibilities: glad, happy, thrilled, and so on.

Scenario #2

In the second scenario, your child is patiently waiting in line when another child cuts in front of them and takes their turn. For best practice, imagine their reaction to this scenario. What do they say, what do they do, what does their face look like? Use the framework and write your reflecting feelings response:

<you> _____
<feeling word> _____
<qualifier> _____
<put it all together> _____

What expressions did you picture in this scenario? I see disappointment in their face. "You are disappointed that you have to wait longer." I could also see frustration: "You are frustrated that you were cut." They might be expressing anger. "You are angry that they took your turn." Imagine looking into their eyes; "You are sad that you didn't get your turn." Each of these feelings could be uniquely expressed by a child. Each feeling has a slightly different explanation to it. Disappointment and sadness are closely tied to the loss of their turn and position. Anger and frustration are more directly connected to the other child. This is a good reminder to let them feel and avoid dismissing their feeling by solving it. Keep it short and let their feeling be the focus.

Scenario #3

In the third scenario, your child missed the opportunity to say goodbye to their best friend before they left on vacation. The plan was to meet after dinner, but rides fell through due to busyness in both homes. They promised each other that they would exchange bracelets but now they will not be able to. Use the framework and write your reflecting feelings response:

<you> _____

<feeling word> _____

<qualifier> _____

<put it all together> _____

This is a more complicated situation and requires some extra thought. As you imagine your child in this situation, what are their emotional expressions? What words are they using, if any? What is their body language, eye contact, and presence telling you? Obviously, their expectations were not met. Disappointment is a very possible feeling. However, there are many more emotions that could be expressed.

"You are angry at me for not driving you."

"You are worried that your friend is upset."

"You are lonely with your friend on vacation."

"You are heartbroken that you couldn't exchange your bracelets."

This is a great scenario to remind ourselves that our kids have real feelings. As an adult, we may not qualify this situation as worthy of anger, loneliness, or feeling heartbroken. We have cognitive abilities and discernment that have not yet developed in our child. However, that does not make our kid's feelings invalid or insignificant. Save yourself and your child from the tendency to solve their negative feeling by telling them that it isn't worth being upset about. They could feel angry at you for not making their plans a higher priority. Sit in it with them before you try to fix it. They may feel worried that their friend is disappointed in them for not making it work. Disappointment is not a wrong answer, it may be the best answer for your child. However, use this exercise to remain open to more possibilities.

Scenario #4

In the fourth and final scenario, your child is playing with a new toy. An alarm goes off and they drop their toy to the ground. What would you say in this scenario? Use the framework and write your reflecting feelings response:

<you> _____

<feeling word> _____

<qualifier> _____

<put it all together> _____

A popular response is, "You are scared because of the alarm going off." This could be a very appropriate and accurate reflection. However, I want to point out a trend that I have noticed in Play Therapy over the years. Children use the word "scared" in their emotional vocabulary frequently. If a situation involves fear, surprise, alarm, shock, or wonder, then I most often hear a child refer to their feeling as being scared. I believe this is evidence of a small emotional vocabulary, both from the child and from the adults who communicate with them. Fear could be the right feeling, but are they actively expressing fear? In your mental image of this scenario, what is the child doing after they drop the toy? Are they shaking, crying, looking at you, looking for the source of the alarm? They may be confused, startled, or surprised by the sound. "You are surprised by that unexpected sound," may be a more accurate observation. My son actually used the term "unexpected" recently. I noted it as a word to add into our emotional vocabulary and use in conversations more often.

TWO NOTES ON REFLECTING FEELINGS

1. **Reflecting Feelings Builds Our Emotional Vocabulary.**
   By practicing with those four scenarios, we were able to identify different feelings and the words that are associated with them. The reflecting feelings skill will influence and grow our connection with our kids, and it will grow the emotional vocabulary within our home. We have mentioned emotional vocabulary several times throughout this chapter and I would like to share more about this concept and why it is so important. We are all born with emotions, but we are not innately given a vocabulary to express them. The formation of our emotional vocabulary begins in childhood. It is not too early for our kids to start processing their emotions and finding the words to express them. By using the reflecting feelings skill, you are modeling emotional vocabulary for them and equipping them to do this for themselves. They may not yet be able to communicate what they are feeling effectively; we need to come alongside them

and help. Reflecting feelings will also help them communicate their somatic symptoms. Somatic symptoms are the physical reactions to emotions that we experience in our body. When we feel butterflies in our stomach, adults immediately recognize that they are nervous, anxious, or worried. When kids feel butterflies in their stomach, they say that they do not feel well. You might hear about a stomachache, headache, or a generic physical ache when a child is really feeling anxious or afraid. You might even take them to the doctor and receive a perfect bill of health. Somatic symptoms are misleading if the child is not able to identify the root cause of their feeling and communicate it to us.

I have had two separate kids try to tell me what they were feeling inside without being prompted. We were engaging in a Play Therapy session when one child just came out and said that they feel "like a spider is spinning a web inside of my belly." If you are a young child with no connection to the phrase "butterflies in your stomach," then you might come up with your own creative interpretation of that feeling. Another child, a little older, told me that they felt like someone stretched out cotton balls inside of their belly. Another delightfully unique attempt at communicating a physical feeling. Children are often dismissed because of their age. I know that many children have shared expressions like these before only to be told that they are silly and to move on. In Play Therapy, I can use reflecting feelings to help them better understand what they are feeling, validate them for having that feeling, and then help them learn how to express it with an emotional vocabulary.

When we use healthy emotional vocabulary, the child's needs are actually met. This is just as true for adults as it is for kids. If a loved one has done something that makes you feel unappreciated, then you may need some comfort and appreciation. However, if you cannot identify and communicate how you feel, that loved one will likely fail to meet your needs. It might be knowing the difference between a doctor visit because they say they feel sick or recognizing nervous feelings and their need to be reassured or encouraged. Thankfully, we know that there is not a spider spinning a web, so that is a straightforward opportunity to engage in reflecting feelings and help better diagnose the feeling!

> *when we use healthy emotional vocabulary, the child's needs are actually met.*

2. **Reflecting Feelings Helps Everyone.** By using this skill, we are meeting an essential need that our children have: to be heard and understood. Reflecting feelings will encourage and validate our children and the emotions that they feel. We are growing the emotional vocabulary of our home and communicating effectively. The fantastic thing is that the principles and skills of Play Therapy are helpful for every generation and people group. This means that the skill of reflecting feelings can be used to better communicate with everyone in your life. I have heard of stories from adults who have used the reflecting feelings skill on an adult friend or sibling. One story was from a person who's sibling constantly complained about a broken leg. They made every conversation about how miserable they were and how their life is ruined due to this temporary setback. Many of us have interacted with someone like this before. The person telling me this story realized that they should try reflecting the feeling that their sibling was expressing.

They reached out to their sibling to say, "It must be frustrating that you are in so much pain. You are angry that you broke your leg and you can't do anything." To their surprise, their sibling softened and calmed down. They changed their tone and stopped complaining; they even offered an admission that they may have been overly dramatic, and that they will make do with their circumstances. Their sibling was feeling frustration and pain, but they were really expressing the need to be heard and understood. By meeting the need for understanding, the sibling could now address their own feelings and regulate how they felt and acted.

We can use the reflecting feelings skill on our spouse, friends, or co-workers. We ought to use this skill to help those around us feel more heard and cared for. Pay attention, watch for cues, and use eye contact. Let your spouse know, "You are feeling unappreciated for what you do for our family." Sit in that feeling with them, see where the conversation goes, and look for moments to encourage and validate. Tell your friend, "You seem so thrilled about that." Honor their feelings and celebrate with them. As you grow in this skill and become more confident in it, try using it on an adult. Everyone needs to be heard and understood, and now you have the tools to meet this need.

PUTTING PRACTICE INTO PLAY

This is the end of the chapter on reflecting feelings, but this is just the beginning of your journey using and growing this skill. We have a proven framework "<you> + <feeling> + <qualifier>," that is our guide to success. We have four tips that will elevate our ability and effectiveness when reflecting feelings. We have had the opportunity to explore and practice this concept through our practice scenarios. Now is the time to put it into action. You are going to build a strong foundation of understanding and care for your child. You are going to be able to relate and communicate with your child on a whole new level. The emotional vocabulary will grow for you and your child as you both discover more ways to share and understand feelings. Be encouraged by something new; you are going to figure this out with practice, and it is going to make a difference. To ensure your success, I encourage you to work on this skill for a week before moving on to the next skill.

For additional practice examples, go to:
devicedetoxbook.com/resources

7 CHOICE GIVING

INTRODUCTION TO CHOICE GIVING

I hope you have taken time to practice our first Play Therapy skill, reflecting feelings. It is a foundational piece of Play Therapy and the Device Detox *Solution*. Each pillar that you adopt is going to support and strengthen the whole structure of what you are doing. With reflecting feelings now in the toolbox, we can set our sights on something new. We are now moving on to our second pillar of Play Therapy, choice giving. The choice giving skill is an essential piece of Play Therapy parenting. I believe that you will come to greatly appreciate this skill; it will serve you well. I know that your child will learn to appreciate it.

Choice giving is the principle and skill that invites children to make choices for themselves. The key is that these choices are made within the parameters and guidelines set by the parent. In a way, choice giving is exactly what it sounds like: the parent allows their child to make a choice. It is a powerful tool that will enrich and empower your child, and it will also uphold your authority as a parent. Children will enjoy being given a choice, which allows them to have a measure of control that they are not normally given. This will create a greater sense of self-worth and identity through their decisions. Parents will experience less struggle and defiance from their kids while also enjoying the benefits that choice giving creates for their kids. When this is done effectively, everyone wins.

Here is a snapshot of how choice giving works. A parent tells their child that it is time to take a bath. The child does not agree, as they want to be in control and they believe that bath time isn't fun. The child declines the invitation to stop what they are doing and head to the bathroom. The parent asserts their power and control by turning off the television in the room and again tells their child that it is time to take a bath. The child, feeling frustrated and powerless, throws a tantrum. This is a battle that has played out countless times. Whether it is taking a bath, going to bed, putting something away, doing a chore, or getting dressed—power struggles happen all the time.

> *parents will experience less struggle and defiance from their kids while also enjoying the benefits that choice giving creates for their kids.*

In this scenario, the choice giving skill could be used to remove the power struggle and achieve the desired outcome. They can invite their child to make a choice between taking a bath after ten more minutes of play or taking a bath after dinner. The parent has set the final outcome and the parameters for their child's choice. The child is given the choice of when they will take their bath, not if they will take a bath. Two things happen as a result. The tension between the child and the parent is alleviated.

Also, the child is less resistant to the final outcome of bathing because they played a part in the decision-making process. In the end, the parent has the outcome they desired, and the child was able to make a choice. Everyone wins.

CHOICE GIVING FRAMEWORK

> **<child's name> +
> <you can choose X, or you can choose Y> +
> <which do you choose?>**

Now that we have introduced this new skill, let's get into the framework of choice giving. You will need to know the framework in order to better understand the skill and effectively exercise it with your kids. The first piece of the choice giving framework is to address the child by their name. The purpose of calling them by name is the same as the "you" in the reflecting feelings skill. Starting with the child's name creates a personal connection and sets the focus on them. Our focus on the kids will help them focus; it will promote their self-awareness and even self-control. Starting with the child's name also helps to establish their role in what comes next.

Now that the child has been personally addressed, we can give them choices. This second part of the choice giving framework goes like this: "you can choose <X>, or you can choose <Y>." This framework signals their role in making a choice; it also signals they are being given a measured transfer of control. They can choose between what we have offered them, choices that direct them to our desired outcome. This framework makes the choice very clear: choice X, or choice Y. The third and final piece of this skill is constant, "Which do you choose?" This reinforces the framework and invites the kids to use the measured control that they have been given.

Now let's put this all together: "<Child's name>, you can choose <X>, or you can choose <Y>. Which do you choose?" This framework is tested and effective; it is the key to using the choice giving skill. These are specific and intentional words that help frame the skill. Parents often insist that they already give choices to their kids. Choices like, "Do you want this, or do you want that?" It may not feel different, but this is not as effective for choice giving. The issue is mainly with the word "want." There are three reasons why:

Reason #1

In life, what you want and what you get are often two different things. Thinking through what you get is a better practice than thinking through what you want.

Reason #2

Picking what you want implies a little more control than they really have. In this process, our kids do need to know that we are giving them options to choose from, not just fishing to meet their wants and wishes.

Reason #3

There is less responsibility in picking what you want. When your child is given two choices and encouraged to take what he wants, you're inviting a less rational decision. When you pick what you want, your attention is diverted to your immediate feelings or perception of instant payoff; it is directed away from a long-term goal or achievement. In the morning, ask yourself: "Do I want to get out of bed early and go for a run, or do I want to sleep-in?" This question is a trap for anyone trying to get into a daily exercise routine. Instead, ask yourself what you choose to do; give yourself more power and balance to make a reasonable decision. These words and formulas matter. At first, our kids may choose what they "want" regardless of whether we use the word "choose." However, we will see the results when we invest in doing this accurately. You can choose to continue doing things the way that you are used to doing them, or you can choose to use this new effective skill. Which do you choose? (See what I did there?) As we prepare to practice using this skill and framework, let's look at three tips to help us succeed.

THREE TIPS FOR CHOICE GIVING

1. **Choices Should Be Age-Appropriate.** When we are using the choice giving skill, the choices we give must be developmentally appropriate. In one sense, we want our choices to be limited based on the age and development of each child. My general belief is that children ages two through seven only need to be offered two choices. Children ages eight and up can typically handle three choices. However, three choices are not always necessary; more isn't always better. We really want them to process their options to the best of their ability, so we do not want to overwhelm them with too many options. Another factor of age-appropriateness to consider is the weight of the choices that we give. For example, a two-year-old does not decide when their bedtime is, we can make that choice for them. An older kid may have some flexibility that allows that to become a choice. Be mindful of your child as you consider how many choices and which choices you provide for them.

2. **Choices Should Be Mutually Agreeable.** We need to make sure the choices we give are agreeable to us. We should never offer a choice that we are going to regret or resent later. Let me give you an example. I often hear about power struggles at the dinner table. Eating a meal is a battle: the child refuses to eat what was cooked, and some form of complaining is involved. This is an excellent opportunity for choice giving to alleviate the power struggle and create a buy-in from the child by allowing them to make their own decision. So, in dinner preparation, the parent could share that there will be a vegetable at the table for dinner and ask the child to choose between two options. The choice is given, "You can choose to have carrots, or you can choose to have broccoli. Which do you choose?" The key here is that the parent is also agreeable to eating carrots or broccoli. Once the choice is out there, it needs to be wide open for the child. So, do not offer broccoli if you hate broccoli! Also, if you know that the child loves carrots and hates broccoli, then this isn't really a choice for them. The second key is coming up with two mutually agreeable choices. Do not try to manipulate your child by offering a choice that you want them to make and then a horrible second choice. I am going to assume the best in you and that this idea never crossed your mind. However, we might be desperate when there hasn't been a vegetable on their plate in over a week; we might be tempted to let them choose between the veggie and a sock! Be strong. Be fair. Be agreeable.

3. **Stick With The Choice.** If your child is not used to this process, they may try to change their choice or back out of it. It is crucial that once the choice is made, we enforce the outcome. Let's say

that while you are making their lunch, you give them the choice to either have an apple with their lunch or an orange with their lunch. They choose the apple. The table is set, and lunch is served. Your child now decides that they don't want the apple, they want the orange. The response, "You are disappointed that you didn't have the orange. You chose to have an apple in your lunch today, so tomorrow you can choose to have the orange." In this response, you have reflected their feeling, you have pointed to the choice that they made for themselves, and you have given them the power to make a new choice next time. There is no power struggle in this response. They have the opportunity to learn and make a different decision; no apology needed from them or from you. You always want to refer back to the choice that was made by the child so that they begin to understand consequences and accept responsibility for their outcomes.

LET'S PRACTICE CHOICE GIVING

Now that we have learned the framework and we have covered the helpful tips, it is time to begin practicing the choice giving skill. We are going to use common scenarios as practice, and we are going to give you space to write out your choice giving response using the framework. After you have written out your own response, we can compare notes as I share my response and a few thoughts behind it. We can use our own kids as the subjects of these scenarios. Picture them, their age and development, and their experience in making choices. Use the formula that we covered. Create agreeable choices that you are satisfied with and that are possible for your child to follow through with. This is a great opportunity to practice with real life inspiration and context. Remember to use the formula:

> **<child's name> +**
> **<you can choose X, or you can choose Y> +**
> **<which do you choose?>**

Let's get started with the choice giving practice scenarios.

Scenario #1

In the first scenario, your child is getting ready for school in the morning. You usually pick out their outfit and set it aside for them as they are getting up in the morning, then you go make breakfast while they get dressed. You can use the choice giving skill to help the getting ready process run smoothly while also empowering your child by inviting them to make a decision. Write your choice giving response using the lines below and afterwards we can compare notes.

_____

_____

_____

_____

My favorite part about this skill is that there are so many appropriate answers. "<Child's name>, you can choose to wear this shirt, or you can choose to wear this shirt. Which do you choose?" Depending on your child's age, the choice might center around the shoes that they wear or maybe the entire outfit. If there is a struggle with getting started in the morning, then I might say, "<Child's name>, you can choose to eat breakfast now, and then go get dressed, or you can choose to get dressed now, and then have breakfast. Which do you choose?" Choice giving can motivate action and drive us towards our desired outcome, while preserving the parent-child relationship.

Scenario #2

In the second scenario, your child is doing homework at the table while you are cooking dinner. There is no power struggle or disobedience going on. You are going to prepare a side dish for the meal and serve it to your family. How could you use choice giving to engage and empower your child?

_____

_____

_____

_____

Let's put this in the context of our own family situation. We enjoy fruit as a side dish, so that is what I'm going to draw from for my response. I want to empower and encourage my son by giving mutually agreeable options and inviting him to make a decision that will impact all of us. "<Child's name>, you can choose for us all to have peaches with dinner, or you can choose for us all to have pears with dinner. Which do you choose?"

Scenario #3

Here is the third scenario. You and your child are listening to music in the car while on the way to a baseball game. This is a common situation for us. How can you use this situation to encourage and empower your child or solve a potential power struggle? Work through this scenario and write out your choice giving response below.

_____
_____
_____
_____

This scenario could potentially turn into a power struggle. A power struggle could form around which songs are played (especially if your fellow traveler wants to listen to the same animated movie soundtrack over and over again). The choices need to be agreeable. "<Child's name>, you can choose to listen to this cd, or you can choose to listen to this cd. Which do you choose?" This is a win for everyone because the kids can pick a new cd to listen to and we don't have to go crazy listening to the same song over and over again.

Now that we have worked through our practice scenarios, let's look at a few notes that will help us better understand and appreciate this skill.

KEY CONSIDERATIONS

TWO NOTES ON CHOICE GIVING

1. **Erase Power Struggles.** In many homes, there are power struggles between parent and child. In reality, kids have little to no power or control over anything. Imagine being powerless over your

own circumstances. You are told where to go, when to go, how to go, and why to go; your opinions, thoughts, and desires do not appear to impact decisions. That is where children sit on the power scale. Kids want more power and control, but they don't have much agency to get it. The voice of the powerless is often unrest. All people who find themselves powerless will try to take control whenever and however they can. Kids operate in the same manner. They will test and exert their will against yours, claiming territory where they believe they can get it. This causes the persistent struggles that arise in my practice: conflicts involving disobedience, not listening, arguing, tantrums, meltdowns, and general non-compliance. In many cases, these behaviors are rooted in a power struggle.

Parenting does not have to be full of power struggles. The beauty of choice giving is that it provides children with a measure of control and power within the appropriate boundaries that we set for them. By using this skill, we allow them a measure of control by letting them make a choice for themselves. We establish shared power instead of fighting over it. Choice giving boosts the value of a child's thoughts and opinions as they are now invited to use them in their own decision-making process. They can exercise their own preferences and personality. As soon as a choice is given, the power struggles begin to decrease in severity. By repeating and honoring the process, your child's appreciation of the power of choice will grow and the power struggles will reduce. The parent does not have to give up their desired outcome; they can offer two options to achieve the end goal and the child is empowered to pick one. That is a balance of power.

Let me clearly explain that you are not giving up total control to your kids, because that is a question that I have been asked before.

"Does this mean that they just get to be in charge all of the time?"

you hold all of the cards in this game, and you get to pick a few cards that they get to play with.

The answer is no—that is far from the reality of choice giving. Shared control through choice giving is a small but significant offering of power to your child. As the parent, you are setting clear limits and boundaries to their choices. You hold all of the cards in this game, and you get to pick a few cards that they get to play with. They cannot generate their own choices or parameters. That role and control remain in your hands. Your kids do not need to have the illusion of being completely in charge of your home. They just need to feel empowered to make a choice that you have given them.

2. **An Investment In Their Future.** Through this process, children are able to grow in their decision-making ability. Choice giving is an investment into our children's long-term problem solving and decision-making skills. This action provides real opportunity to learn and grow. Unfortunately, most kids do not have a healthy variety of opportunities for decision-making. That lack of experiences often carries into high school or college, which means young men and women are entering adulthood with little experience or confidence in making choices for themselves. They are missing valuable training and practice. While they are children, they get to practice in the safety net of the parameters set by the parent. As an adult, there are not many parameters or guidelines for their decisions. The best time to safely practice decision-making is in childhood. By giving children these opportunities, you are investing in their futures.

One result of choice giving is that our kids learn to embrace the consequences of their own decisions; they build character and accountability. They learn the valuable lesson that "with great power comes great responsibility." Choice giving equips them with a measure of control. They also learn that how they use that power matters. Every choice has a consequence, and every consequence is a teachable moment. They are learning to accept the consequences of their decisions, good or bad. These lessons will prepare them for life and carry into their future. Choice giving is a skill that will impact your children now, and will set them up for success in the future.

PUTTING PRACTICE INTO PLAY

Now that you have had some time to learn and discover the skill of choice giving, it is time to begin using it at home. As you prepare to do this, I challenge you to start by identifying the best opportunities to give choices. What are the areas where you routinely decide everything for your child? What does giving choices look like in those scenarios? Where do you experience power struggles? What does giving choices look like in those scenarios? I encourage you to rehearse it in your mind and practice communicating the choices. Use the reflecting feelings skill to start. Let them know that you see their frustration or that you see their potential, and then move into choice giving. Reflecting feelings can help set the stage for choice giving; practice using them together.

This is the second of three Play Therapy skills. From here, we will move into the limit setting skill. Then we will be able to put them all together to reduce screen time. Remember that each skill plays a part. Continue to practice reflecting feelings. Now, introduce choice giving. Go slowly. Be patient with yourself. Know that everything will grow and build as we go. I am so excited for you to build this second skill! You are going to become more and more confident in your skills as you remain committed to them. This is going to make a difference in the life of your family and the future of your kids. I encourage you to work on it for a week before progressing to the third and final skill in this book.

For additional practice examples, go to:
devicedetoxbook.com/resources

8 LIMIT SETTING

INTRODUCTION TO LIMIT SETTING

Welcome to the third and final Play Therapy skill of Device Detox. There are four pillars of Play Therapy, however, this is the last one that we will utilize for *The Solution*. We have covered the reflecting feelings skill and the choice giving skill. Now, we can bring in the limit setting skill. This is the one that parents typically want me to start with because they see a connection to discipline. We have the greatest urgency to correct behaviors and establish order in our home. Limit setting will help us do that! After all, you cannot correctly execute limit setting without first installing the reflecting feelings skill and the choice giving skill. You will see that the third cannot exist without the first two. We have been building our *Solution*, one piece at a time, and here is where it starts to come together.

Here is a quick review. The intention behind reflecting feelings is to help children feel heard and understood. The choice giving skill helps children feel a measure of control and empowerment by exercising their decision-making muscles. They are both incredible and vital skills on their own. You have already been exploring and growing in your ability to use them. Limit setting utilizes the first two principles and adapts them into an effective form of discipline. Discipline is a hot topic and one of the top concerns among parents and caregivers. We all want to know that we are being effective and handling situations appropriately. When the need for correction presents itself, we want to be sure that we are prepared to do it effectively. Limiting setting will help us achieve consistency, fairness, and confidence.

This skill first acknowledges and reflects the feeling that a child is expressing. It then limits unacceptable behavior, and it gives the child a choice to express their feelings in a more appropriate way. Here is an example: Inside the home, there is a "no yelling" rule. One of the kids is angry and goes off, yelling and stomping around the house. It is essential to start with the child's name, to clearly and personally address them in this moment. It would go like this: "<Child's name>, I know that you are upset right now. The house is not for yelling in. You can choose to <alternative way to manage their anger that you are comfortable with>, or you can choose to <alternative way to manage their anger that you are comfortable with>. Which do you choose?"

Their feelings have been acknowledged. The limit of no yelling in the house has been set. The choices were given to take alternative action that is more appropriate. Notice how the communication was calm and neutral. It does not directly attack the child, it does not dismiss their feeling, and it doesn't invite an argument. The response could have been, "I told you to stop yelling because…" This would pit the parent against the child. Stating the limit, "The house is not for yelling in," is something that can be said very calmly. It is like saying that the grass is green outside. It does not require an emotional response, a snappy response, or a critical response. Parental authority does not come from volume or posturing; it comes from setting clear limits. Clearly, this behavior is not acceptable, so alternatives are given. As we discussed in the last chapter, the options have to be agreeable. The parent needs to identify preferences that they are comfortable with. So, if one alternative is "you can choose to go outside and yell," then that choice needs to remain a realistic option for them. Reflect their feelings, set the limit, and give alternative choices that are agreeable. The combination of these is limit setting. Just stating the limit will not address the child's feelings or invite them to make a more appropriate choice. Limit setting meets all of the needs of the child, while enforcing the desired outcome for the parent.

> *parental authority does not come from volume or posturing; it comes from setting clear limits.*

THE LIMIT SETTING FRAMEWORK

reflect the feeling + set the limit + give the choices
^
"the <subject> is not for <behavior>"

Just like the first two skills, limit setting has a framework to follow. First, there is an internal framework for limit setting that communicates what the limit is to our children. Then, there is the final limit setting framework that puts it all together into its full form. Both frameworks are vital for effectively using this skill. We are going to start with the internal framework that allows us to clearly and effectively communicate the limit: "the <subject>

is not for <behavior>." We begin with the subject, which is the focus of the framework. This might be a household item, a time of day, a specific room or place, a person, or whatever it is that we are communicating the limit for. This subject is not meant for the behavior that it is experiencing. So, we say, "the <subject> is not for..." followed by the behavior that needs to be limited. The behavior is addressed in regard to the subject; the subject is the focus, not the child, and not the parent. This framework does not create any criticism or judgement. It is clear and matter of fact. "The <subject> is not for <behavior>."

With this unique piece now covered, we can add all three skills together to create the full limit setting framework. We start with the reflecting feelings skill because this is where we always start. Our kids need to be heard and understood and this is our first step in the framework. We address our child and reflect the feeling that is at the root of their behavior. Remember, kids have an emotional center, so their behavior and expressions are emotionally driven. We reflect the feeling in order to establish our understanding of them and help open the door for their own self-reflection and self-regulation.

Next, we communicate the limit that has been set. "The <subject> is not for <behavior>." The child's emotions are driving behavior that is not appropriate for the person, place, or thing. We are calmly stating the fact that this subject is not for the behavior that it is receiving. "The food is not for throwing," or "The Play-Doh is not for eating." We are communicating to the child that the behavior needs to change to fit the limit, or the desired outcome for the subject. The change is not going to be driven by punishment; it will be offered as a choice.

The third and final piece of the framework is choice giving. After the limit has been set, a more appropriate choice can be made. "You can choose X, or you can choose Y. Which do you choose?" The child now has two agreeable options that fit the limit and desired outcome of the parent. All together, it looks like this: "You are upset that you lost your game, but the house is not for yelling in. You can choose to stop yelling and continue playing, or you can choose to go outside and yell. Which do you choose?" The child is being heard and understood while also being empowered to make a decision. Meanwhile, the limit is being honored and the desired outcome is achieved. Now that we have covered the framework necessary for this skill, let's look at three important tips that will help us be more effective when using the limit setting skill.

KEY CONSIDERATIONS

THREE TIPS FOR LIMIT SETTING

1. **Think Through The Limits.** Limit setting needs proper thought and attention; it shouldn't be rushed or an overreaction. We might prematurely issue a new limit when it isn't completely necessary. Children already have a long laundry list of "do nots," expectations from authority figures, and, of course, the things that they must do. The Play Therapy model is not meant to pile onto that list needlessly. We only set limits for things that are necessary, which we have specifically seen and need to address. It is worth thinking through whether the specific action or behavior is worth creating another limit. In my Play Therapy sessions, the kids come in with no rules. We set the limits as we go. If one child colored on their arm with a marker, then that child receives a specific limit in response

to their particular action. The other children are not debriefed at their next session and updated on the new company policy. Each child is given limits as personal interactions to them and the specific behaviors that they have expressed.

Another helpful way to think about limit setting is whether it is corrective or redirective. In other words, we can use limit setting to correct a child's behavior, but we can also use it to redirect a child's behavior before correction. Corrective means that we enter at the point where discipline is required. Redirective means that we are more preemptive, making an attempt to educate and influence the behavior before it escalates. We don't want to wait until behavior is out of hand. Limit setting is a tremendous redirective tool, pointing children to those agreeable alternatives and helping them make more appropriate choices. When correction is needed, limit setting will help address and correct the behavior. It serves us in both situations.

2. **Be Calm And In Control.** The second tip for limit setting involves your volume and tone. For the most effective limit setting, be patient and use a calm, firm voice. I know that not all of us always remain patient and calm. Some of us have a tendency to yell, maybe even overreact. Some people have a tendency to match the tone and volume of the person they are talking to, including their kids. When we embrace this skill, we learn that we do not need to overreact or yell. We do not need to escalate when the child escalates. We simply need

> *we do not need to escalate when the child escalates. we simply need to be calm and assertive.*

to be calm and assertive. The energy that we communicate with is extremely important. If we sound nervous, our kids will pick up on that. If we sound confident, they will feel that too. It is crucial to remain neutral and in control. By modeling this for our kids, we are helping them build the same characteristics in themselves. We want our kids to be well adjusted, calm, and confident. This posture will serve you well and it will serve them well.

3. **Get On The Same Eye Level.** The third limit setting tip is to get on the same eye level as your child. I remember a great illustration on this subject. A husband and wife were having some marital issues and needed to work some things out. The husband was a huge guy, around 6'5" and 250lbs; the wife was about 5'2" and really petite. In therapy, the wife explained that she always felt like her husband was talking down to her, being condescending and aggressive. That was her perception. The psychologist saw an opportunity to address this. She drew a circle on the ground and had the husband sit down in it. Then, she had the wife stand up on a chair in front of him. The psychologist told her to say to the husband all of the things that were bothering her. She also told her to do this in a stern and angry voice. The husband quickly understood the position of being smaller and what it felt like to be talked down to. He understood that the dynamics of their sizes play a role in how they perceive and receive the other person's communication.

You are likely taller than your kids. It certainly depends on your circumstances; I have been confronted with the troubling reality that my son is getting closer and closer to my height! I am with those of you who are almost there or those who are now looking up at

Limit Setting

your child. But for the majority of this parental collective, we are physically looking down on our children. Our communication and limit setting is most effective when we adjust our eye level to their eye level. We can sit, kneel, or squat—it doesn't have to be one form or another. <u>Meeting your child's eye-level is so helpful in reading their emotional state and balancing out the dynamic between you.</u> We are meeting them where they are, establishing a connection. This is really important for limit setting.

LET'S PRACTICE LIMIT SETTING

Now that we have learned the framework and covered the helpful tips, it is time to begin practicing the limit setting skill. We are going to use common scenarios as practice, and give you space to write out your limit setting response utilizing the framework that has been provided. After you have written your response, we can compare notes as I share my response, and a few thoughts behind it. Once again, we should use our own kids as the subjects of these scenarios. Picture them, their age and development, and choices that would be mutually agreeable in your home. Use the formula that we covered.

reflect the feeling + set the limit + give the choices
^
"the \<subject\> is not for \<behavior\>"

Scenario #1

In this first scenario, you have two children that are starting to get on each other's nerves. One of your kids starts screaming at their sibling after their toy was taken from them. How can you use the limit setting skill to support and guide your screaming child? Use the framework and write your response on the lines below:

_____
_____
_____
_____

We need to start with the feelings. What feelings are you reflecting back at your child? Now, what is the neutral limit for your home? And what are the choices that will be given? I might say, "Jack, I know that you are frustrated that your sister took your toy, but your sister is not for screaming at. You can choose to come tell me that she took your toy and let me handle it, or you can choose to ask her to give it back. Which do you choose?" Those choices are in line with my desired outcome, and I'd prefer either of them in the future over screaming.

Scenario #2

In this scenario, you are working on a project at home. It could be a work project, a home project, a cleaning project, or whichever project suits you. Your child wants to play and is persistently asking you to play with them. How could you use the limit setting skill in this situation? Use the framework and write your response on the following page.

_____
_____
_____
_____

This is an interesting scenario. I might say, "Jack, I know that you are excited to play a game but this time is for work, so my next hour is not for games. You can choose to sit with me and wait to play a game later, or you can choose to find your sibling and play a game with them right now. Which do you choose?" By explaining that I am working on a project, I have stated a neutral fact about what is happening. This is more of a redirective situation. Even though I found a way to incorporate this framework, it isn't entirely necessary to use the "[subject] is not for [behavior]" phrase because I am not trying to make any long-term limits or corrections. My kids can patiently wait with me or they can find another person to play with.

Scenario #3

In this third scenario, your child is holding a marker in their hand. They are looking at the wall and then glance over at you to see if you are watching. Now they are looking for your reaction to what we all know is about to happen. They make eye contact with you and then quickly look back at the wall. How do you handle this situation? Use the framework and write your response on the lines below.

_____

_____

_____

_____

There are several approaches based your scenario. I might say, "Jack, I know you want to color right now, but the wall is not for coloring. You can choose to color on some paper, or you can choose to color on the sidewalk with some chalk. Which do you choose?" I could also flip the limit setting phrase into a more positive form by saying, "The marker is for coloring paper." This is still a calm and neutral truth with a slightly more positive spin on it. I just wanted to share that, in case you want to expand your phrasing just a little bit.

Scenario #4

In this scenario, your child starts to kick a soccer ball in the living room around your fragile decorations. The potential for broken or damaged goods is all too real. Use the framework and write your response on the line below.

_____

_____

_____

_____

I might say, "Jack, I know you enjoy kicking the ball, and you are having fun, but this area is not for playing soccer (or the ball is for outside—the more positive reverse of the phrase). You can choose to kick the ball outside, or you can choose to find a different toy to play with in this room. What do you choose?" The feeling was reflected, the limit was set, and the choices were given. We were able to validate their desire to play and have fun without crushing that feeling. At the moment, our concern could be for the safety of the decorations, and we might unintentionally dismiss their desires for play. The limit setting skill helped us calmly place a limit on their behavior without having to limit their passion and interest.

Scenario #5

In this final scenario, your child wants to go play at their friend's house. However, it is close to dinnertime, and the meal is already being prepared for everyone to enjoy together. Write your response on the lines below.

_____

_____

_____

_____

I might say, "Jack, I know that you love spending time with your friends and that you are excited to go to your friend's house, but this time is for our family dinner. You can choose to try and see them after dinner, or you can choose to see them tomorrow. Which do you choose?" Are you starting to feel comfortable with this skill? Keep practicing!

A NOTE ON THE BENEFITS OF LIMIT SETTING

There are so many benefits to these principles of Play Therapy. They all begin to overlap and overflow through your new parenting powers. Just like in choice giving, limit setting also helps kids learn to self-regulate. Our use of limit setting and choice giving provides opportunities to practice self-control and self-regulation. They can make choices and learn from the consequences, positive or negative. Lots of places have rules to follow, but limit setting provides the intentional space to grow in a healthy environment.

Imagine how a parent responds when their child is yelling at them. The parent explains that they do not want to be talked to like that. The child continues to yell. The parent insists that the child needs to calm down. The child continues to yell. The parent now threatens punishment, explaining that the child will be in trouble if they do not stop. The child carries a little further until the parent has had enough and the consequence is enforced. This is a common and consistent pattern for dealing with behavior. However, what do you think the child learned from this situation? They learned where the line was, or at least where it was this time; the line could be different next time. They discovered that they can keep pushing until the point of correction. What if the parent asked three times and then counted to three in order for the child to stop? Well, the unintended outcome is that the child learns that listening is not important until the counting starts.

Limit setting helps kids self-regulate and learn self-control. It presents them with other options to consider and choices that actually have weight. As with choice giving, the culmination of this skill will result in lifelong benefits in the development of the child. Finally, limit setting creates a healthy balance of power. They are given a measure of control, under the established parameters and limits, and can freely operate in the space that they have been given. Parents get to be clear and kind. Kids get to be understood, are empowered to make choices, and will learn to embrace consequences.

PUTTING PRACTICE INTO PLAY

You have learned the principles and frameworks of three Play Therapy principles. You now have three amazing tools, ready to use and share with your family. This chapter wraps up our *Solution* and leads us to *The System*.

This is what we've been leading up to this whole time. You embarked on this journey to specifically address screen reduction and the issues surrounding screens. We have covered a lot leading up to this point. I would encourage you to make the practice and implementation of these skills a priority. There are multiple benefits from the skills that you have learned. Continue to invest in them as doing so invests in your child's future. These skills may still feel unknown and uncomfortable, but stick with them. The confidence will come, and things will start to click. Reflecting feelings, choice giving, and limit setting are the essential tools to achieve device detox. You have made it so far already; we are getting closer to the end. Thank you for taking the time to learn and explore the world of Play Therapy. Next, we will unpack *The System* to reduce screen time and the battles that surround it. You're almost there! After you practice and become more confident in using the limit setting skill, we are ready to jump into *The System*.

For additional practice examples, go to:
devicedetoxbook.com/resources

SECTION FOUR:
THE SYSTEM

9 PUTTING IT ALL TOGETHER

Welcome to the Device Detox *System*! We want to arrive at a healthy amount of device use; that is the reason why you started reading this book in the first place! So, we will work to scale back to whatever that amount is for your family. We desire a kind and peaceful transition, but we understand that there will be struggles. We intend to prevent the outbursts and tantrums that come with reducing screen time. Kids are used to large amounts of screen time, and some are addicted to it. We need to remember *The Science* involved and consider that emotional and behavioral reactions to reduced screen time are to be expected. The good news is that we have *The Solution* and *System* to help us lead healthy change for our families. We have the right skills to enter this arena with confidence and strength. We have every tool that we need. Now we can apply these skills with structure and purpose as we apply them all together in the Device Detox *System*.

We have learned three Play Therapy skills: the reflecting feelings skill, the choice giving skill, and the limit setting skill. These make up our Play Therapy-based *Solution*. Now we are ready to put it all together and effectively reduce screen time and the struggles regarding device usage. In this chapter, we are going to activate our skills in new ways. The new focus of our training, practice scenarios, and conversation will center around reducing screen time.

DEVICE DETOX SCENARIOS: REFLECTING FEELINGS

This section is going to help us practice using our skills by working through common scenarios surrounding screen time. Before we get started, we need to recognize and celebrate that we have flexibility in the Device Detox *System*. Flexibility is not often an option when implementing a new system. When we try something new, there is a tendency to revert back to how we've done it in the past. Play Therapy and the Device Detox *System* give us options! We get to explore as we practice and expand our choices as we go. The best way that I solve a scenario may be different from the way you solve a scenario. For each of us, we may discover a different way to use our skills the next time we face the same scenario. That is what I love about this process. We can evaluate each moment and determine which combination of skills we need to achieve our desired outcome. It invites us to customize and personalize our approach to *The Solution* and *System*.

I don't want to sound like a broken record, but I do want to reflect for a moment. You can have more than one phrase or word to reflect a feeling; remember, our goal is to grow our emotional vocabulary. You can have a variety of agreeable choices to offer your child. You can use choice giving to address a power struggle or to simply treat your kids to some valuable and empowering decision-making opportunities. You can choose to set a limit or not. You can craft limits to meet the specific needs of your household. Take advantage of the personal capabilities that Play Therapy provides. Your children will feel more heard, understood, and empowered when we personalize our approach.

Let's take a look at some scenarios and use our Play Therapy skills. This time, the scenarios are going to be Device Detox-based. We will start by focusing on the first skill, reflecting feelings. Examine the scenario and write your response on the lines below. I will share my thoughts so that we can compare notes. Remember to use the framework:

<you> + <feeling> + <qualifier>

Reflecting Feelings Scenario #1

In the first scenario, your child has been asking all day to have more time on their tablet. They are obsessively asking over and over again. Occasionally, they demand to have it instead of asking for it, whining when their request is denied.

<you> _____

<feeling word> _____

<qualifier> _____

<put it all together> _____

What feelings could be behind their behavior, and how do you reflect them back to your child? I might say, "You are upset that you cannot watch more of your show," or "You are excited to play your game again."

Reflecting Feelings Scenario #2

In this scenario, your child is given twenty minutes of screen time before it is time to stop. The reason for stopping could be dinner, bedtime, or simply a timer that you set to limit their screen time. Pick whichever reason best fits for you, or mentally practice them all. The twenty minutes are up, the device is turned off, and your child is not happy.

<you> _____

<feeling word> _____

<qualifier> _____

<put it all together> _____

Imagine the non-verbal cues, their expression and demeanor. What feelings are being expressed? I might say, "You are frustrated that your screen time is over," or "You are mad that I asked you to turn it off." In this scenario, several attempts at reflecting feelings may be needed, and then there could be an opportunity to use our other skills as well. We should always recognize and validate their feelings before rushing into action. In every scenario, we need to prioritize this foundational skill. It is very possible that the reflecting feelings skill is all that was needed to address this scenario, and we can determine if limit setting and choice giving are necessary or not. This is where we get to uniquely craft our response to each situation.

DEVICE DETOX SCENARIOS: REFLECTING FEELINGS + LIMIT SETTING

Let's go ahead and use this last scenario to practice adding another skill. We are now adding limit setting on top of reflecting feelings. We reflect the feeling, and we set a neutral limit. Use the lines below to write out your response. We are going to combine the two skills and use the proper framework. Remember, the limit setting framework is:

> **"the \<subject\> is not for \<behavior\>"**

Reflecting Feelings + Limit Setting Scenario

In this scenario, your child is given twenty minutes of screen time before it is time to stop. The reason for stopping could be dinner, bedtime, or simply a timer that you set to limit their screen time. Pick whichever reason best fits for you, or mentally practice them all. The twenty minutes are up, the device is turned off, and your child does not want to stop.

\<reflecting feelings\> _____

\<limit setting\> _____

\<put it all together\> _____

Our desired outcome is that they turn the device off and transition to whatever comes next. We use "this \<subject\> is not for this \<behavior\>" to make a clear and neutral limit. It is clear and neutral because it is a statement of fact, not a personal judgment or inconsistent opinion. No one can argue that the time is up. This combination might sound like this: "You are angry that your screen time is over, but this time is not for playing games." We could also use the limit to reinforce the desired outcome. "You are annoyed that your screen time is over, but it is time for dinner." One more response: "You are excited to watch more of that show, but your screen time is up for today." The combination provides an understanding of how they feel and the opportunity for them to regulate their feelings in response to hearing the neutral limit.

DEVICE DETOX SCENARIOS: REFLECTING FEELINGS + LIMIT SETTING + CHOICE GIVING

So far, we have combined two skills in order to respond to device and screen time. Now, let's add choice giving into the mix. We are offering mutually agreeable choices to empower the child and enforce the neutral limit. We are going to use the same scenario once again; this will help us build each skill on top of the other. Use the framework for each skill and write your response on the lines below. I will share my thoughts and responses so that we can compare notes. Remember the choice giving framework:

<child's name> +

<you can choose X, or you can choose Y> +

<which do you choose>

Reflecting Feelings + Limit Setting + Choice Giving Scenario #1

In this scenario, your child is given twenty minutes of screen time before it is time to stop. The reason for stopping could be dinner, bedtime, or simply a timer that you set to limit their screen time. Pick whichever reason best fits for you, or mentally practice them all. The twenty minutes are up, the device is turned off, and your child does not want to stop.

<reflecting feelings>_____

<limit setting>   _____

<choice giving> _____

<put it all together>   _____

Time for the full combination. I might say, "You are frustrated that your time is up, but now it is time for dinner. You can choose to continue playing this game again tomorrow, or you can choose to use your time doing something else tomorrow. Which do you choose?" Their feeling has been acknowledged, the limit of screen time is reinforced, and they are empowered to choose how they want to use their time tomorrow.

Reflecting Feelings + Limit Setting + Choice Giving Scenario #2

Here is a real-life example from my personal experience. We went over to a friend's house on a weekend. Our son loves to play video games with his friend. While he was visiting our friend's home, he was allowed to have one hour of tablet time. When that time was up, he didn't want to stop playing. Our son, like most kids, is an expert at stalling. His time to play had run out, but somehow the tablet was still in his hands. He began to negotiate, and stalled for a little more time. Before we realized it, that 60-minute session was just expanded to 70 minutes. (Another time he worked it to 76 minutes!) Using the skills that we have learned, how could we respond in this situation?

<reflecting feelings> _____

< limit setting> _____

<choice giving> _____

<put it all together> _____

Once we fully adopted these skills, our response to this scenario changed. I would now say, "You enjoy playing games with your friend, but your time is up. You can choose to stop playing now and have your full amount of time when you come over again, or you can choose to continue playing and lose your tablet time for the next time that you come over. Which do you choose?" The options are clear and the choice is his. The limit has been clearly set and the outcome of his actions and decisions are totally his own. I will enforce the outcome that he chooses. In these moments, we know that our kids may not respond to the set limit or the choices that we have given them. But this is where ultimate choice giving comes into play.

INTRODUCTION TO ULTIMATE CHOICE GIVING

We need to address those moments when our kids do not accept our limits and throw tantrums. You may have been wondering about this type of response. There is a solution and skill for these moments and it is called the ultimate choice giving response. Ultimate choice giving is used in the most difficult arguments and negotiations. Here is what it looks like. We give the child three opportunities to comply. This means going through the process of reflecting feelings, setting limits, and giving choices three times. Give them space to process and react each time. Choices need time; do not rush the three opportunities. A child can take up to sixty seconds to process a decision. Let's take a moment to reflect on how this would look in real life. Slow down your reading and play this moment out in your mind: You have just given the first opportunity to regulate their emotions and make a more agreeable choice. Your child continues to yell and demand more screen time. Let the moment sit, do not lose control or match the child's energy. Give the second opportunity with time and space for your child to process the choices and respond. Your child continues to yell and swings into a full tantrum. Give the third

choices need time; do not rush the three opportunities.

opportunity for your child to respond, maintaining full sincerity and patience.

I understand that parents desire their child to respond quickly without having to repeat themselves. The goal is not for us to force obedience. The goal is for the child to choose to obey. That is why they are given three chances to comply with the choice, and that is also why we provide them with time to really process what we are saying. Avoid jumping in to force the tablet out of their hands or turning the television off before they have time to process the request. Forced obedience is not truly obedience, because they never accept the result or learn to control and regulate their emotions. Also consider that swift enforcement without time for the child to process is rarely done in a calm and neutral manner. When we jump in, we put the responsibility of what happens on ourselves and not on our children's choices. This can unintentionally cause a step backward.

> *the goal is not for us to force obedience. the goal is for the child to choose to obey.*

If they have not complied after the third request, then you can move into ultimate choice giving. This response offers a clear option between a positive choice and its positive outcome, and a negative choice and its negative outcome. We need to provide both options to the child; do not leave one of the options out, assuming it is implied. Be clear and direct with what the two options are and what their corresponding outcomes will be. The ultimate choice sets the table for our kids to make a decision and for the chosen outcome to be enforced. The outcomes must be agreeable, just as we discussed with choice giving. They will receive the result that they choose. Either choice will offer a valuable learning opportunity through its outcome. This is a heavier form of choice giving but it holds the same benefits. This step will assist in growing their decision-making abilities. It can empower them by providing a measure of control. Ultimately, these choices settle the power struggle by setting up a valuable decision with a significant outcome. There is a specific framework that will help us give a clear and consistent response when implemented.

ULTIMATE CHOICE GIVING FRAMEWORK

> "If you choose \<positive choice\>, then you choose \<positive outcome\>. If you choose \<negative choice\>, then you choose \<negative outcome\>. Which do you choose?"

Now that we have some understanding of what ultimate choice giving is and what it does, let's look at the framework for putting it into practice. "If you choose \<positive choice\>, then you choose \<positive outcome\>. If you choose \<negative choice\>, then you choose \<negative outcome\>. Which do you choose?" This framework is consistent and clear. The communication is directed to the child, placing them as the focus. The choice is also directed to the child, empowering them to make a decision. The decisions have a clear connection between the choices and their outcomes. Everything is set for the choice to be made and the outcome to be reinforced.

The framework requires the choices to contain value. We need to identify what currency is valuable to our kids—this will help us create valuable choices and consequences. What motivates them? What matters to them? What is significant to them? These things become the incentive to choose the positive or negative outcome. There should be an understood value at play when making this decision. That value is either going to be gained or lost, depending on the choice that is made. By ending the framework with "Which do you choose?" we are once again placing the power and responsibility of the outcome in the hands of our kids. If the value is dessert after dinner, then they can choose to have it or lose it. In the next chapter, we are going to build an incentive system that will further empower our kids. Identifying value and currency for our kids is vital to the impact of the ultimate choice giving framework and to establishing an incentive system.

KEY CONSIDERATIONS

TIPS FOR ULTIMATE CHOICE GIVING

1. **Enforce The Agreeable Choice & Consequence.** As the parent, we provide the desired outcome, identify the currency, and give agreeable choices. The child gets to exercise control through making the choice. Afterwards, the parent honors their child's choice by enforcing the outcome that they chose. Following through is critically important. We should be calm, firm, and clear. They do not get dessert if they chose not to get it earlier. They do get extra screen time

   whatever the consequence is, positive or negative, we need to see it through.

   if that is what they chose earlier. We cannot change our minds or back out of enforcing the consequence. Whatever the consequence is, positive or negative, we need to see it through. If, in hindsight, we change our minds about a choice that was given, then we need to be sure not to offer that choice next time. If the consequence that they chose was not to have any dessert, then we can expect them to be sad when dessert time comes, and they do not have any. We can reflect their feelings and then remind them that this was their choice for now, but next time they can make a different choice.

2. **The Consequence Is Enough.** We should be comforted to know that the consequence is enough. We do not need to belabor a negative choice and consequence. If their friend asks, "Why don't they have their tablet anymore?" we can just explain that our child chose not to have it for the weekend. If they cannot have dessert, we can explain to their siblings that they decided not to have dessert. In these moments, the consequence is enough. We do not need to shame our child, embarrass them, or make them tell other people what they did wrong. We have the power to influence our children with hope and potential with the words we choose. I might say, "He chose to leave the park early today, but he is going to try again next time." They can make a different choice next time. They are not bad kids; they made a choice that had negative consequences. They will grow and learn to make more effective choices in the future.

3. **Choose Five Times.** When you use the ultimate choice giving phrase, you will use the word "choose" five times. All five times are important. Your child will learn that their choice is what allows them to gain control of their circumstances. Yelling, throwing fits, and disobeying is not going to bring any positive consequences or currency to them. It will be hard. It will test your patience and

confidence. We cannot expect them to grasp the concept of what is being offered immediately. They will likely need to see it played out a few times before they understand. They will grow in self-control, self-regulation, decision-making and problem-solving skills. These moments of awareness come when we make it very clear that they are choosing the outcome. "If you choose A, then you choose B. If you choose C, then you choose D. Which do you choose?" makes it very clear where the responsibility lies—with the child.

LET'S PRACTICE ULTIMATE CHOICE GIVING

Now that we have learned the framework and covered the helpful tips, it is time to begin practicing the ultimate choice giving response. We are going to use common scenarios as practice, and we are going to provide you with space to write out your ultimate choice giving response utilizing the framework provided. After you have written out your response, we can compare notes as I share my response and a few thoughts behind it. Once again, we can use our own kids as the subjects of these scenarios. Picture them, their age and development, and choices that would be mutually agreeable for your home. Consider the currency of value that will bring their decision-making opportunity into focus. Use the formula that we covered.

> "If you choose <positive choice>, then you choose <positive outcome>. If you choose <negative choice>, then you choose <negative outcome>. Which do you choose?"

Scenario #1

Imagine that your child screams and yells at the screen while they play video games. (Some of us do not need to work hard to imagine this.) You've already set the limit three times with little to no response from your child. How would you handle this using ultimate choice giving? Come up with your reflecting feeling, limit setting, and now the ultimate choice giving options. There was a choice given for the first three times, but this is the first time that the ultimate choice is given. Take a moment, write your response on the lines below.

\<reflecting feelings\>_____

\< limit setting\> _____

\<ultimate choice giving\> _____

_____

\<put it all together\> _____

_____

I might say, "You are angry that you lost, but inside the house is not for screaming. If you choose to continue yelling inside the house, then you choose to end your time playing video games for today. If you choose not to yell anymore, then you choose to continue playing until your time is up. Which do you choose?" The options are clear, the limit is set, and the child can choose the positive or the negative consequence. Okay, let's look at another one.

Scenario #2

In this scenario, your child's thirty minutes on their tablet is up, and they are resisting the limit. You have set the limit three times; there was no progress. I believe that you have a great handle on the first skills, so let's go right to the ultimate choice giving. Use the lines below to write out your ultimate choice giving response.

<ultimate choice giving> _____

_____

I might say, "If you choose to stop right now, then you choose to keep all thirty minutes for tomorrow. If you choose not to stop right now, then you choose not to have thirty minutes of screen time tomorrow. Which do you choose?" When we begin to reduce screen time, losing a thirty-minute block is a huge deal. In other words, that is valuable currency. It often takes making that negative choice once in order to feel the weight of it.

Scenario #3

In this third scenario, your child wants to use your phone to watch their favorite show at the dinner table. You are looking to limit screen time, and the dinner table is not a place that you would like for kids to have any devices. A device-free table is your desired outcome. Your child is starting to complain and refuses to eat their food. The limit has been set three times. How would you use the ultimate choice giving skill to address this situation? Write your response on the lines below.

<ultimate choice giving> _____

_____

I might say, "I know that you want to watch your show, you really enjoy it, but the dinner table is not for devices. If you choose to sit with us and eat your dinner, then you choose to have dessert with us after dinner. If you choose not to eat dinner, then you choose not to have dessert with us after dinner. Which do you choose?" The device coming to the table is not an agreeable choice because it directly goes against our desired outcome. I want to make a tangible and immediate choice, so I chose dessert after dinner to be the focus of my positive and negative consequence. The child's desire is the show they like to watch, and I recognized that feeling. However, I pointed them to the limit and offered them something else as a choice.

ONE NOTE ON ULTIMATE CHOICE GIVING

Give Grace, Receive Grace

As you take steps to implement this approach towards the issue of screen time, be prepared for some struggles. Parents typically have a good sense of how situations will play out. We can all be surprised at times, but we often have an accurate idea of how our kids will react to something. As you imagine some of these scenarios playing out, I suspect that you see trouble ahead. Some of you are following the framework we have laid out so far: we reflect our child's feelings, we set a limit, and we give choices, and they still refuse to do what they were asked to do. Friends, this is a real and possible initial reaction to leading change in your home. You are going to present these three skills of Play Therapy beautifully, and there will still be moments of rebellion.

Do not be disheartened by this. Our kids have not had this type of practice with self-control and self-regulation; they will likely struggle with it at first. This will be as brand new to them as it is to you. However, they have not been given tools to learn or practice ahead of time, as you have. You are coming into this with more experience and knowledge than they are. We can give them time to process and recognize these principles. Be patient with yourself as you learn and prepare to do this. And be patient with your children and give them some grace as they encounter these concepts and choices for the first time. Give yourself some grace too. You are learning and practicing something new. You deserve grace, and they do too.

THE BEGINNING OF THE END FOR DEVICE ADDICTION

We are officially turning a corner in our struggle against screen time and device addiction. We have learned proven skills. We have trained and practiced applying those skills in a variety of scenarios, including scenarios that involve devices. We are beginning to bring our knowledge and skills home and put them into action. This is likely what you came here for, and the time has come to really give it your best shot. Your journey forward may get off to a rocky start, but forward progress will carry you to the places that you want to go. Step by step, limit by limit, choice by choice. This is the beginning of new confidence and strength in your parenting. It is the beginning of greater control and regulation in the heart and mind of your child. Even if your child doesn't respond immediately, the groundwork is being laid for them to take massive steps of growth. Remember why you are doing this. Know where you are headed and believe that you are already on your way there!

10 BUILDING AN INCENTIVE SYSTEM

We are almost at the end of Device Detox! We have come a long way together, and the final pieces are falling into place. We have covered three principles and skills from our Play Therapy-based *Solution*, applying them to our Device Detox mission. We are beginning to reduce screen time, power struggles, and tantrums. Through every effort and practice, we are growing confidence and competence in our abilities. Even in our struggles, we are growing and learning. You are putting it all together and building a system that is going to work for your family.

If you know anything about me, you know how much I LOVE baseball. It is one of my three favorite things, after my husband and son. We cheer for the Tampa Bay Rays and love going to games. I often think about how applicable baseball lessons are to so many other areas of life, and incentivizing children based on their currency is no exception. If you follow baseball at all, you might be familiar with the story of Roy Oswalt. Roy played for the Houston Astros and was an ace pitcher. In the pennant race against the St. Louis Cardinals, Roy was told that if he clinched the victory, he would be given what he had always dreamed of. But to know the rest of the story, we have to go back to spring training of 2005. Every year, Drayton McLane (the Astros' owner) asks his players what their goals are. In that early-in-the-season meeting, Roy replied that he wanted to own a bulldozer. Roy comes from a small town in Mississippi and owns a 1,000-acre ranch with his brother. Ever since he made the majors several years before, he wanted a bulldozer to repair two lakes and build some roads on his property. So, in the clubhouse before that game, Roy was incentivized—win and you'll get what you've always wanted. And win he did. In December, he received a Caterpillar D6N XL from the Astros, complete with a huge red bow on top. While we are not dealing with professional athletes or shelling out thousands of dollars for tractors, we can look at how baseball teams harness incentives to help the team achieve their desired outcome. The same principle applies with our kids!

INTRODUCTION TO INCENTIVE SYSTEMS

We are going to utilize incentive systems to help us achieve our Device Detox goals and win as a family. This is going to be a fun and rewarding system that will complement and reinforce the Play Therapy skills you are already using. You will develop and personalize your system, and you will love the benefits that come from it. Not only will this help you regulate screen time, it will also help reinforce and support many other desired outcomes for your kids and for your family. An incentive system is a healthy and practical tool for you to develop with your kids. It empowers parents and children, elevating the motivation for making choices. It promotes intrinsic motivation: motivation that comes from within yourself, not from or for someone else.

The incentive, or currency, of screen time is valuable. In a business sense, the currency value of screen time increases as available screen time in the market decreases. Science tells us that screen time needs to be limited for children. We need to be careful that we are not rewarding too much screen time, as that would be counterproductive to our mission (and would inflate the value of the screen time as an incentive). However, you are the best person to understand and identify what currency will be effective for your child. Screen time will be used to illustrate our four systems so that you can practically reduce the amount of screen time in your home. After you have conquered the Device Detox plan, feel free to explore other options to incentivize your kids about different issues unrelated to screen use.

In this chapter, we'll unpack four successful incentive systems. My husband and I have used different methods depending on our son's age and development. We tweaked each one and changed them to fit our son as he matured. When you implement one or more of these systems, you will see the benefits, but please understand that implementing these involves time and dedication. These techniques require trying them more than once. I hope you test them out a few times to give them time to take root. I encourage you to make the necessary adjustments that bring out the best results for your family. Let's take a look at some tips that will help you effectively build and facilitate an incentive system in your home.

KEY CONSIDERATIONS

FOUR TIPS FOR BUILDING AN INCENTIVE SYSTEM

1. **Determine A Healthy Amount Of Screen Time.** We are going to use our systems to help us reduce screen time. To begin, we need to decide what a healthy amount of screen time should be. Determining a healthy amount of screen time involves several factors. One major factor is age. Younger kids and older kids can handle different amounts of screen time. Another factor is the child's reaction to screen time. Screen time impacts each child differently; some have stronger responses to it than others. Overall, it comes down to what each family feels comfortable with and what works best for their family. It may have better results to choose a particular time of day or days of the week that are predetermined. For example, we could allow thirty minutes of screen time right after school or one hour per day on the weekends. It may be better to have an allotted amount of time for each day so the child can have some influence on when they would like to use it. This is another opportunity to customize and explore your options.

   Everyone needs to make their own determination about screen time. However, it is essential to know what experts think. The American Pediatric Association, the World Health Organization, and a number of other organizations and agencies have weighed in. The general consensus is that children ages 0-2 should not have any screen time. Toddlers should have limited to no screen time as well. Children between the ages of 4-10 should have no more than one hour of screen time per day. That is one total hour, across all devices. In other words, sixty minutes of screen time combined from the computer for schoolwork, television, tablet, phone, and video games. Children who are eleven years or older can have up to two hours per day.

> *sixty minutes of screen time combined from the computer for schoolwork, television, tablet, phone, and video games.*

2. **Measure Their Screen Time.** In chapter four, you were asked to "draw a starting line" by identifying where your child was in daily screen time use. Let's do that exercise again; it is valuable. Take a moment and do your very best to add up your child's daily amount of screen time. Make sure you add up all of the platforms. I am curious if this amount has changed since chapter four. Either way, there is a good chance that your number is higher than the recommended amount. I strongly encourage you to consider those recommended amounts of time for your family. You certainly have the freedom to allow a higher amount if it is safe to do so, but that is gauged by each child's reaction to screen time.

   Take the daily amount that you just measured and compare it to the amount that you desire to have going forward. Do not be intimidated by the difference. You have the skills to get you from here to there. Soon you will also have a system that will reinforce and support your journey. It is essential to know how far you have come, and identify where you need to go. Continue to actively measure screen time. This will help you accurately and effectively incentivize your kids. If they are accessing more screen time than you realize, then you may be over incentivizing them. Also, if you do not have a sound system for measuring screen time, then you will have a hard time enforcing the consequences. Remember: If they chose to lose screen time, they cannot get it later because you forgot that they lost it or decided to give them a break on the consequence. Likewise, if they chose to earn screen time, they must be able to use it. Either scenario undermines the choice that they made and it makes the incentive system less effective. <u>Set everyone up for success with a planned and purposeful system for keeping track.</u>

3. Clearly Explain The New Expectations & System.

The system will give you the tools that you need as long as you communicate it well. Our family made the decision that devices are only allowed on the weekend. Our son can choose to earn screen time throughout the weekdays and then he can cash in the time that he earned over the weekend. No, we do not have any screen time from Monday through Friday, across the board, for all devices. Our system allows our son to earn up to two hours on Saturday and two hours on Sunday, for a total of four hours per week. That was a choice that we made as a family. Obviously, you can (and should) make a decision based on what is best for your family. You can set up a daily amount for all seven days, or you could have a smaller amount for weekdays and a larger amount on weekends. You could have certain days with no screen time and counter balance with days with heavier usage permitted. You may allow screens for homework everyday but limit which days or times of the week they can watch television. I suggest having a daily and weekly amount in mind, and then schedule accordingly.

Whenever you are ready, you will need to sit down and explain the new expectations to your child. Provide the new limits and times in an honest and clear way. Give them age-appropriate insight into the fact that unlimited screen time is not good for them. Reflect the feeling that you understand how much they enjoy it, and explain that your family needs to do what is best to take care of each other. Everyone loves dessert, but we cannot allow each other to have dessert for every meal of the day; it would make us sick. The new screen policy is going to be what is best for the whole family. The expectations need to be clear so that they can make the best decisions for themselves. If the new plan is for one hour per day, then they need to know that getting on their tablet puts them on the clock. Perhaps you chose to have two hours a day but in 30-minute increments. Whatever the details are, make them clear and communicate them to your kids. Have them say it back to you to make sure they understand. If you have multiple children, you may have more than one limit to communicate. If your oldest child gets more screen time than the younger one, communicate that clearly as well.

> *reflect the feeling that you understand how much they enjoy it, and explain that your family needs to do what is best to take care of each other.*

4. **Identify The Incentives.** The last tip for success is to use incentives in your screen time management system. Incentives are a beneficial tool and powerful piece of your system. Incentives build an investment and work ethic for your kids. They are participating in the system to gain more currency. The system starts by defining your time limits and expectations. Then we are going to build around the desired outcome to create a full system that supports and facilitates your family's goals. Determine what your incentives are going to be. Using screen time is a trendy option, especially for the kids who were just told that they will be experiencing significant cuts in daily screen time. A chance to earn some amount would be a comforting and exciting incentive. You know what will connect with and motivate your child in the best way. At this point, you have your time limits and schedule picked out, you have communicated with your kids, and you have determined the best measure of incentives for rewarding positive choices. You are ready to put these pieces together and create a system.

SYSTEM #1: THE BOARD SYSTEM

About The System

This first system is called The Board System. This is a behavior modification system. We can use the Board System to address one or two of the biggest behavioral issues with which you and your child struggle. Imagine what your life will look like when those issues are resolved. This system helps focus on that one thing and provides positive reinforcement to correct it. It uses a positive reinforcement model, which means the child earns something that they want for doing the behavior that is desired. I read an article recently that stated toddlers hear the word "no" around 400 times per day. That communication clearly focuses on negative behavior. A positive reinforcement model positions us to catch our children doing good and incentivizes them to repeat it. Witnessing this transformation is fun and rewarding for parents.

How It Works

To operate this system, you will need a board. Any type of board that you can write on will do just fine (whiteboard, chalkboard, etc.). There are lots of board options to explore for this system. Once you find your board, you will want to place it in a prominent location that is easy for your kids to see. You will need a marker or anything that will show a clear mark on the board. In this system, your child will receive a mark when they express the targeted behavior that you have chosen. Focus on one or two of the biggest behaviors that you would like to see changed. If there has been a struggle with yelling, then the desired behavior to incentivize is to play without yelling. Make it clear what the target behavior is and what they will be earning if they do it. Use marks on the board as an acknowledgement that the child did the thing that you would like them to do. Each mark has a value, or currency, attributed to it. If your incentive system value is based on screen time, then earning a mark could mean earning five minutes of screen time. You can set up your system to pay out the incentives at the end of every week, on the weekends, or at whatever time you establish. Be clear in the expectation for behavior, the rewarding of the mark, the value of the mark, and the payout structure for earned marks.

> *a positive reinforcement model positions us to catch our children doing good and incentivizes them to repeat it.*

It is critical to pay attention to your child and honor their positive behavior with a mark. They may be excited and ask for marks when you did not notice their behavior. To the best of my ability, if I believe that my son did the right thing, then I go ahead and give him the mark. Even when he is fishing for it, if he does the positive behavior, I give him a mark. The whole point is to incentivize the positive action and empower our kids to make better choices. The board is based on a balance of positive reinforcement and holding your child accountable for counterproductive behavior. If they do decide to express the negative behavior, then a mark can be removed from the board. I might say, "Because you chose to yell during playtime, you have chosen to lose a mark."

Organizing The Board

It is helpful to organize your board. It is especially beneficial if you are looking for two different behaviors. If one behavior is not yelling during playtime and the other is not complaining at the dinner table, then have a clear way to mark each specific behavior. You can set up rows and columns on your board. The rows can signify a particular behavior, and the columns can represent days of the week. This can help you organize your board and prevent missing or doubling marks that are earned. It also clearly shows your child what they are being incentivized for. They can look and see that, while they have not yelled each day this week, they have missed three days of not complaining at the dinner table.

Organizing the board will also help demonstrate your pay out method and time. Monday - Friday, our son can earn screen time to be used on the weekend. Organizing our board with days of the week helps us keep an accurate account of his earned incentives and helps him see how much time he has earned or missed through the week. There are less discrepancies when the board is organized well.

Work The System

Do what you need to do to personalize the system and make it work for you. You may use a dry erase board with colored markers. You may use a chalk board with white or colored chalk. If you have more than one child, you can use one board with different colors, or you can develop a board for each kid. There are many options and you can choose what works best for you. You can begin with one behavior to modify, or you can try two. I recommend keeping the focus on one or two behaviors at a time so that it is not overwhelming or difficult to keep track. If you feel the time has come, you can switch your targeted behaviors to something new. I encourage you to explore the Board System and learn how to best utilize it in your home.

SYSTEM 2 : THE CHART SYSTEM

About The System

The Board System was behavior-based; it focused on behavior, attitude, and communication. The Chart System is a task-oriented system; it focuses on actions, tasks, and chores. By using this system, we are incentivizing tasks to be completed. Some examples include putting your dishes in the sink, making your bed, or doing your homework. The chart system reinforces the desired outcome of an action. Perhaps you have seen potty training charts, chore charts, sticker charts, and so on. To operate and facilitate this system, you will build a chart. The chart will inspire desired tasks to be completed. The tasks are given an incentive that relates to whatever currency or value that you have established. Each task has a specific value that is earned when the task is completed.

How It Works

To set up your chart, you will first need to determine what your desired tasks are. The number of tasks and the tasks themselves should be age-appropriate. We can use the examples of putting the dishes in the sink, making your bed, and doing your homework. Each task has a clear predetermined value. For a task-oriented system, you can base the value on how frequently they can do the activity and how difficult it is. You can also weigh their interest in doing the task. If making the bed is an enormous struggle, then consider making the bed a more valuable task. It will make sense to them; they have likely seen task charts in other places. I would explain that this chart represents behaviors and actions that are valued and rewarded with points. Explain to them what the tasks are and be very clear on what the expectation is for each task. Children are infamous for having their own ideas of what cleaning their room looks like, so help them out by giving them some specific expectations. The chart clearly shows which tasks have been completed. This could be done with a marker or pen. It could be shown by placing a sticker next to the task.

Here is a quick story to illustrate how we used our chart. We have a 25-minute drive to school each day, so we give our son his breakfast in the car. This helps him get more sleep each morning. We noticed that he would not start eating his breakfast until we were three minutes away from school, so he never finished it. We realized that this was an excellent opportunity to use the chart system. We explained to him that we are adding breakfast to his chart, and if he eats his entire breakfast before we get to school then he gets points for it. It empowered him to make a choice, helped him eat his breakfast, and eliminated a daily struggle for our family. He ate breakfast, which was our desired outcome, and he got to earn a little more screen time, which was his extrinsic motivation.

Organizing The Chart

This is a task-oriented system, so the tasks on your chart should be well-organized. It needs to be clear which task is being acknowledged and incentivized when you place a sticker, marking, or writing on the chart. You can set up rows and columns on your board to help demonstrate the tasks and the amount of times that they have been completed. Once again, you will need to decide when and how your child can redeem the incentives that they have earned. At the end of the week, they can tally up what they have earned to use over the weekend, or they can use it anytime, as long as they don't use too much in one day. Clearly communicate the value and the mechanism for using the incentives that they have earned.

Work The System

There are lots of chart systems out there. This can provide some inspiration and ideas for how to organize and facilitate your chart system. You could do the chart system on a board—that doesn't make it a board system. (Board systems are behavior-based and chart systems are task-oriented.) You can use paper and create a whole new chart every week, if that works best for you. Work the system to fit your needs and the needs of your kids. Tasks for the chart need to be age-appropriate; a five-year-old and a ten-year-old are capable of different tasks. They are also capable of a different number of tasks over a given period of time. It is helpful to have a different chart for each child. Take the necessary time to plan out the tasks that fit your child, assign the value of the tasks, and determine the timeline and incentive mechanism for your chart. Communicate all of this clearly and enjoy watching your child complete tasks with excitement!

SYSTEM 3: THE BANK SYSTEM

About The System

The Bank System is fun and unique. This is a teaching tool and a task-oriented system. It was actually developed out of our passion to teach our son some lessons about personal finances. There are limited ways for children to develop skills and understanding with money, banking, and saving. So, we stumbled upon this thought and ended up developing this system as part of an incentive program for device use. We have had a lot of fun with it, and I encourage you to give it a try. I suggest that this system be used for children ages seven and up. However, that is your judgement call.

It doesn't take a lot of resources to get started. The Bank System is simple and effective. Being a task-oriented system, we are once again focused on activities, tasks, and chores. The examples are the same: putting your dishes in the sink, making your bed, or doing your homework. The language of the incentives and the mechanism for using them are what make this system special. Instead of marks, stickers, or points, the kids are earning "money." The money goes into a "bank" and they can take money out to spend it on screen time, or whatever the established incentive is.

How It Works

First, you will need a list of tasks and their corresponding monetary values. As we mentioned with the last task-oriented system, each task needs a clear expectation and appropriate value. The second thing that you will need is a bank. This is a place to record the amount of money that has been earned and deposited. When tasks are completed, the money earned gets put into the bank. The options for the child are to spend the money by taking it out of the bank or save the money by leaving it in the bank. We did not encourage the idea of using cash or a wallet; we did not want to practice having money on hand. Instead, we found an old check book and taught our son to write checks when he wanted (and was allowed) to spend his hard-earned money. Explain all of this to your kids. Have them repeat it back to you in order to build confidence that they understand.

Organizing The Bank

Organizing your bank will be a fun project for your family. This is an educational opportunity. Parents, you can get as creative as you would like when making your bank. For us, the bank was a number written on a board in the kitchen, which kept track of his earnings and current balance. The payment mechanism was a checkbook that he could use to write a check to purchase extra screen time. Like I said, it doesn't require a lot of resources to work this system. Our checkbook belonged to a closed account, so we felt comfortable letting him use it. If you do not have something like that at home, there are practice checkbooks that you can order online if you want to try that method with your kids. Obviously, it is very important that you do not lose the bank. I would recommend opening a note in your computer or phone to keep track of deposits and withdrawals. It is satisfying for the child to be able to ask what their balance is and receive a quick answer. We coached our son through writing checks and how to make the amount payable to us. You may want to keep notes with transactions to look back later and see that x amount came in for this task or x amount was spent for this amount—the ledger is helpful for this. You probably won't get audited, but keeping tidy books is good practice for us and will help hold our banking system accountable to our kids.

Work The System

With a unique and creative system, we ought to have some fun. Explore different options for your bank and for your payout system. Consider the age and development of your kids. We view this system as an educational tool, so think about how you could set up your kids to learn from this system as well. Consider what you need to maintain and organize your bank. If tasks become too mundane, consider adding a fresh new task as an opportunity to earn more money. I encourage you to explore the Bank System and learn how to utilize it in your home best.

SYSTEM 4: THE GARMIN VIVOFIT JR® SYSTEM

About The System

This is the fourth and final system that I would like to share with you. This is a system that we created using the product, Garmin Vivofit Jr.® We are not affiliated or sponsored by this product in any way. We stumbled into this product with no anticipation that it would become a part of our Device Detox system. A friend of ours has a son who loved the watch, and they told us about it. We researched it, liked what we saw, and we bought one. We quickly realized that this watch has an app that works very well for the reward system. I need to specify that there are two different watches, the Garmin Vivofit® is for adults and the Garmin Vivofit Jr® is for kids. The kids watch has some special features that inspired us to create this system. I recommend that this system is best for ages seven and up. But again, that is your decision to make.

This is also a task-based system: activities, achievements, and chores—all the same examples. What is so remarkable about this watch is that it functions as a bank system. When a child completes a task, they can immediately see the result on their watch. There is an app with a virtual piggy bank, so when our son completes a task, he can see coins going into his virtual bank. There is often a delay in the other systems; you might have to wait until you get home to add a mark to the board, sticker to the chart, or note in the bank. There is a mobile app that parents can download and pair to their child's watch. That is how the parent can give easy and instant rewards to their kids. They can earn coins based on things that they do and tasks they complete. They can also cash in their coins from their watch or the parent's phone.

How It Works

The initial set up is the same as the bank system. You need to develop the list of tasks, the value for the tasks, and the payout mechanism that allows them to use the incentives that your kids have earned. Then you explain this all to the child. They need to know that the new watch is going to help keep track of the fantastic things that they do. We can show them the piggy bank and explain how they can earn coins. We need to discuss the expectations for each task, so they understand how to earn them. The function is pretty similar to the Bank System, but everything happens virtually on their watch through the parent app. The parent app controls all of the settings, tasks, value amounts, and tracking system. Whatever you adjust from the app will instantly update for your child to see.

Organize The Watch

The parent app allows us to put custom tasks right on their watch. It also allows us to create values for completing a task. We can see that the current tasks allow our kids the potential to earn x amount of coins. The rewards could be 15 coins for fifteen minutes of video games, or 30 coins for thirty minutes of television. We can see how many they currently have and which tasks they have completed. It really is impressive. We took the systems that we had been facilitating on paper and whiteboards, and we brought it to this mobile setting. I encourage you to check out the Garmin Vivofit Jr.®

Work The System

Once again, this needs to be an age-appropriate system. There are still lots of things to customize, including the watch itself. The watch has a variety of bands to choose from. Your kids might love to pick out their own watch band. That in and of itself can be a reward for them if they earn enough points, or dollars, in the virtual piggy bank. There are a lot of features to explore on the watch. I encourage you to explore the Garmin Vivofit Jr® System and learn how to best utilize it in your home.

ONE NOTE ON SETTING UP A SYSTEM

These four systems have all impacted and encouraged our family. We have had a lot of fun developing and tweaking the various nuts and bolts of each system in order to serve our needs and personalities best. I would love to know which of these systems are the most interesting to you at this moment. Which will you try first? Which one best fits the age and development of your kids? We have done them all, and we learned a lot about operating an incentive system through the process. So, I would like to share a little more advice with you in order to set you up for success.

When developing your incentive system, it is vitally important to consider how much screen time you feel comfortable giving your child. Through this process, you are awarding value that can be used to earn more screen time. If you give out too much value or if the price of screen time is too low, then you may find yourself indebted to a savvy child who earned themselves ten hours of screen time in one week. Earning an extra ten hours of screen time in a week is hopefully above what you feel comfortable giving to your child. There needs to be a balance between how much currency can be earned and how much screen time can be bought.

Let's say that you want to offer a maximum of two hours of earned screen time. You can consider using a 1:1 ratio, points per minute earned. With that ratio, you would want to make sure that your child cannot earn more than 120 points in one cycle. If you're going to keep the numbers low, then you could use a 1:5 ratio, where 1 point earns them 5 minutes. With that ratio, you would have to make sure that your child cannot earn more than 24 points in one cycle. Also, if you are working with a banking method, then you will want to establish a guideline for the maximum amount of points that can be spent in one cycle (per week, or per weekend, or per day depending on your system). Your child may be shockingly frugal at first and store up a massive wealth of points. Allowing them to cash in 500 points at once would be counterproductive. Establishing balance in a productive system means establishing a spending limit for the bank. No matter which system you use, be thoughtful in your approach to currency and earning screen time.

EXPLORING THE INCENTIVE SYSTEMS

We are using our skills to relate to and guide our kids through the difficult shift of Device Detox. Reducing screen time is not easy for anyone. These incentive systems reinforce the limit of screen time. They support our decision to only allow certain amounts of screen time at certain times.

It maintains our desired outcome and provides a measure of control and excitement for our kids. They can choose to earn more of what they want when they choose to behave and act in a positive manner. Each system is really a tangible expression of choice, played out right in front of us. It will benefit the Device Detox process now and continue to build good decision-making skills and self-regulation skills for the future.

We have four options because there is not a one-size-fits-all system for incentives. Work the systems to determine what best serves your family. You will likely come to a point when you are ready to switch to a new system, and that's great! Go through the process again, set yourself up for success, and communicate the new system to the best of your ability. Your kids will be thankful that they had a personalized experience and receive positive feedback and attention. Think about that for a moment. These systems put you and your child in a position to encourage and support each other mutually. Cherish those opportunities to learn and grow together, encouraging each other along the way.

> *each system is really a tangible expression of choice, played out right in front of us.*

We have gotten some feedback from parents who have used series of systems, and have been told that, with several children all in different age ranges, it can be difficult to manage multiple charts or banks all at once. In this case, these parents created a hybrid system of several components from each option to make it work for them; you can do this too! One mom allowed an hour of screens in the morning and an hour of screens at night for positive behavior. Her children could earn those hours according to compliance with household rules, but they could also lose those hours for fighting, disobeying, etc. Make this work for you and your family, based on your needs and your kids.

Several families mentioned that the Device Detox process worked well for them when they cut off screen time entirely for their kids for several weeks and then worked back up to a healthy amount using the system. Because the children in these cases had a severe addiction, they felt it was necessary to remove all screen time instead of reducing it. Again, this is a case by case decision, but you can start from zero and build, or scale back depending on your kids and your desires.

> For examples and printable charts, go to:
> **devicedetoxbook.com/resources**

11 DISCOVERING THE RESULTS

When I think of discovery, I think of great explorers. But, to a lesser degree, I also think of contestants. Years ago, there was a minor league baseball game near us in Clearwater, Florida. The home team was giving away a car to one lucky contestant at the end of the game. They picked nine fans from the stands and brought them down onto the field. A bucket with nine keys in it sat next to the brand new car. The contestants lined up, and, as the bucket passed down the line, each fan reached inside to take one key. Starting at the front of the line, the contestants were invited to enter the car, and whoever held the key that started the car was the winner. The excitement in the stands began to build as the first seven keys did not start the vehicle. The eighth contestant was visibly excited, jumping up and down and smiling ear to ear. She knew that she had a 50/50 chance of winning this car, and seemed confident that she was going to win. She jumped into the car and turned her key in the ignition…and nothing happened. She had lost. At this point, the ninth contestant on the field realized that he had won by default. His celebration erupted, along with the crowd's cheers.

Contestants get one shot to win that is often influenced by the circumstances more than their determination or skills. Explorers, however, are investing in discovery on an entirely different level. Explorers have a vision for something that hasn't been fully seen or realized. They prepare and practice their skills in anticipation of the journey ahead. It takes great dedication and strength of will to embark on an adventure for discovery. The heart of every explorer holds a vision for the future and a trust in skills to get there. Being from Florida, I have enjoyed the history and the mystery of explorers that have traveled to and from this land. Sailors, pirates, missionaries, refugees and treasure hunters have sailed across our waters for centuries. A vision of something new, something better for their family drove these explorers here. Their skills were developed and trusted so that the dream could be made real. These people were inspired and confident enough to step onto the boat, setting sail across the water for a new destination. Discovering the outcome of where they would end up would take time and perseverance.

All explorers encounter obstacles while on their journey. The beginning of a journey has anticipated struggle and resistance. Getting the ship out of the dock and out to open waters takes adjustments and maneuvers. It takes trust to work through those early frustrations. <u>Trust that you are doing it right, making the right adjustments, and learning as you go.</u>

My story is full of struggles, waves, and bumps. I have made so many adjustments through trial and error. It took thinking and practicing, tweaking and fixing, until I started to gain momentum and speed. True discovery isn't an overnight journey. Trust the skills and process. Hold on to the vision and promise of your destination. Parents are explorers, too! Device Detox is a new and exciting adventure that you have already begun to pursue. You have the vision of a healthy and happy home where your children are not impacted by overexposure to screens. You have the skills and the systems to navigate these waters and discover the results that you seek.

THANK YOU FOR TAKING THIS JOURNEY WITH ME

I want to pause and celebrate with you! <u>Look how far you have come and look at everything that you have learned.</u> I hope you find a way to encourage and celebrate yourself for all the time, energy, and effort that you have put in. Our Play Therapy *Solution* and Device Detox *System* has a proven track record of success. Your hard work is paying off, and it will continue to be a blessing to your entire family. Thank you for taking this journey with me. Thank you for being a part of this and for trusting me to share my research and Play Therapy principles. I appreciate you taking the time to listen to my story, because that is no small thing. Sharing stories is one of the most beautiful and ancient ways to create bonds between people. I sincerely hope to hear your story one day. At the very least, I hope that you find ways to share your story with someone who could grow and learn from it.

There are more ways to hear from me and my continuing journey with Play Therapy and the Device Detox *System*. You can discover my blog and website www.thekidcounselor.com, where I have shared many articles and stories from my experiences at home and in private practice. I have a Youtube channel, www.youtube.com/kidcounselorbrenna, that you can subscribe to in order to hear and see more of my presentations and research. I also have a podcast - "Play Therapy Parenting," available on most major podcasting platforms (apple, google, etc.) Connect with me in those locations, I hope to have the opportunity to interact with you and hear your story.

I also want you to know that there is a companion video training that goes along with this book. It has extra information and illustrations for Play Therapy skills and the four incentive systems. Go to www.devicedetoxbook.com for more information and additional resources. Until then, I want to give you some encouragement and some final thoughts as we wrap up this book.

KEY CONSIDERATIONS

THREE KEYS TO SUCCESS

1. **Believe.** I have invited you to try and explore a lot of new things. You are using these new skills that you've learned: reflecting feelings, choice giving, and limit setting. You are exploring new systems for reducing screen time and incentivizing positive outcomes. I have mentioned several times that it is most appropriate and helpful to remain calm, be neutral, and try not to react with your own emotions. While that is a true and useful ability, I do want you to know that you still need to be yourself through all of these practices. Be confident in yourself. Believe in yourself. Sometimes things are going to be hard. Sometimes things are going to be frustrating. Don't get defeated. I know that you can get up and try again. That is what we all must do. It will get better. Don't give in, even if it feels frustrating. Even if it feels like it's not going the way that you had hoped. Don't quit; keep going. Persevere. You can do it. Believe that you are confident and competent enough to handle it, and that you

have what you need to be successful and effective.

Believe in your kids, believe in their ability to change. Believe in their ability to regulate, to learn, grow, and work within these new systems and skills that you are bringing into the family. Motivate yourself to continue even when things aren't working out; even when you are frustrated. Stay strong. Go back to the skills, and remind yourself what you've learned. Believe in yourself, your kids, and your skills. You will discover the results as you maintain consistent practice and believe with hopeful anticipation. Trust me, I have seen a lot of families work through a lot of things. You are not alone in this. Everyone is capable of more than they realize. That is true of me, you, and our children.

> *believe in your kids, believe in their ability to change.*

2. **Be As Prepared As Possible.** You have a child, or multiple children, at home and under your care. They are counting on your parenting and principles to guide and protect them. As natural and expected obstacles arise, we can trust the process and be patient. The other side of the coin is that we need to be as prepared as possible! If you picked up this book and went straight to this chapter to "discover the results," then you are not alone. You are looking for answers and results that are going to help your children. You care about them and you want what is best for them. Let me reflect on your feeling for a moment: "You desire to be a good parent." Congratulations, you are!

We are good parents who need better tools. Device Detox and Play Therapy offer us better tools. If you flipped to the back of the book or read through it as quickly as possible, then you should go back and reread it. If you never paused to practice with the scenarios, then you ought to go back and give it a try. Turbulence is expected; we know it is going to be a struggle, especially in the beginning. Our best response, our best gift to our children and to ourselves, is to be as prepared as possible. Every time we are about to begin a new Play Therapy skill, we need to do our best to be prepared. Reread that section or chapter of the book. Find additional resources. Use mental repetitions and work it out in your mind. Revisit the tools and skills again if you still feel unsure.

There is no rush. I understand that you want to see results.

> *our best response, our best gift to our children and to ourselves, is to be as prepared as possible.*

That is a normal and healthy feeling. However, you will get better results when you are prepared. You may want to take a few days to review each skill and implement them one at a time. Remember, they build on each other. Investing quality time to prepare your reflecting feelings skill will pay dividends through the rest of your skills. The incentive systems will be most effective once the three Play Therapy skills are in place. All of this takes time, it takes focus, and it takes intentionality. When we are as prepared as possible, we honor ourselves and our children. You're not successful because you do it perfectly. You're not successful because you figured it all out right away. You're successful because you try.

3. **Be Personal.** My family has used this system for years. We have tweaked it as we've gone. You have seen the variations of the

systems that we've put in place. We did not start with four different systems for incentives, we built them. Those four systems each have massive potential to be personalized, customized, and adjusted to best serve your family. The principles and the skills have concrete and scientific reasoning behind them. However, that doesn't mean that you can't make each skill and system personal.

The skills have concepts and formulas that I insist be kept. For example, starting with the child's name or "you," and saying the word "choose" five times in the ultimate choice giving phrase. Those are principle-based aspects of Play Therapy and Device Detox. It is up to you to contextualize and personalize the communication. Be wholly and freely yourself. You are going to say and do things that you probably wouldn't have said or done before you learned these skills. However, you can still be authentically you. Your kids need you to address them specifically, and they need you to address them as yourself.

The aspect of choice giving is an excellent example of why being personal matters. If you just copy my examples and my "I might say" responses, then you are giving them words that were meant for someone else. That isn't as helpful or rewarding for either of you. It certainly was not my intention when I provided my examples in this book. I trust you to operate with the confidence and brilliance that you have, and to be uniquely yourself through this process. I trust you to empower and invest in your kids by giving them personalized focus through your communication. All of these personal pieces matter. It's going to shape your relationship with your kids and impact the way you view yourself as a parent. You are telling a great story with your life, and no one is better at telling it than you.

SHARE THE RESULTS

You came here for three reasons; three truths that speak to your heart and your intentions. You want what is best for your children, you desire to be an effective parent, and you want to grow as a leader for your family. We shared the goal of reducing tantrums and behavioral struggles, especially as they relate to screen time. We covered three Play Therapy skills and four incentive systems that will help us accomplish all of these goals. As you continue forward on your journey, you will continue to discover and experience the benefits and results of Device Detox. You will continue to develop and grow confidence and competence in your skills and your systems. You have already come so far.

> *you are telling a great story with your life, and no one is better at telling it than you.*

You are now an explorer and pioneer in this arena, so I challenge you to share your experience and your results with others. My first great joy was discovering how to apply *The Science*, *Solution*, and *System* to change my family's story from struggle to success. My second great joy has been to share my experience and the things that I have learned with other parents. You are telling a great and compelling story with your life. Your onward journey with Device Detox is an adventurous tale that other people will want to hear. It will spark a vision for others to pursue a happier and healthier home and effectively reduce screen time for their kids. You are now part of a growing movement, and your voice is a valuable part of the message.

I am so thankful to be a part of your journey. I am grateful for the time and effort that you have put in for your kids. Connect with us online and share updates on your progress. I know that you will be successful. I look forward to hearing all of the great things that come out of Device Detox in your home.

And remember: everything is connected and all of your successes are birthed in your relationship with your children. Nothing else has as much of an impact! Happy relationship building.

REFERENCES

- Aliyari, H., Sahraei, H., Daliri, M. R., Minaei-Bidgoli, B., Kazemi, M., Agaei, H., Sahraei, M., Seyed Hosseini, S. M. A., Hadipour, M. M., Mohammadi, M., & Dehghanimohammadabadi, Z. (2018). The Beneficial or Harmful Effects of Computer Game Stress on Cognitive Functions of Players. Basic and Clinical Neuroscience Journal, 9(3), 177–186. https://doi.org/10.29252/nirp.bcn.9.3.177
- Alter, A. (2017). Irresistible: The Rise of Addictive Technology and the Business of Keeping Us Hooked. Penguin Books.
- Aria, B. (2008, January 14). How to Say No (Without Saying No). Redbook. https://www.redbookmag.com/life/mom-kids/advice/a2560/how-to-say-no/#:~:text=The%20average%20toddler%20hears%20the,parents%20offer%20more%20positive%20feedback
- Christakis, D.A., Zimmerman, F.J., DiGiuseppe, D.L., McCarty, C.A. (2004). Early Television Exposure and Subsequent Attentional Problems in Children. Pediatrics, 113(4), 708-713.
- Dunckley, V. L. (2015). Reset Your Child's Brain: A Four-Week Plan to End Meltdowns, Raise Grades, and Boost Social Skills by Reversing the Effects of Electronic Screen-Time.
- Garrison, M. M., Liekweg, K., & Christakis, D. A. (2011). Media Use and Child Sleep: The Impact of Content, Timing, and Environment. Pediatrics, 128(1), 29–35. https://doi.org/10.1542/peds.2010-3304
- Kabali, H. K., Irigoyen, M., Nunez-Davis, R., Budacki, J. G., Mohanty, S. H., Leister, K. P., & Bonner, R. L. (2015, December 1). Exposure and Use of Mobile Media Devices by Young Children. American Academy of Pediatrics. https://pediatrics.aappublications.org/cgi/doi/10.1542/peds.2015-2151
- Kardaras, N. (2016). Glow Kids: How Screen Addiction Is Hijacking Our Kids - and How to Break the Trance. St. Martin's Press.
- King, D. L., Gradisar, M., Drummond, A., Lovato, N., Wessel, J., Micic, G., Douglas, P., & Delfabbro, P. (2012). The Impact of Prolonged Violent Video-Gaming on Adolescent Sleep: An Experimental Study. Journal of Sleep Research, 22(2), 137–143. https://doi.org/10.1111/j.1365-2869.2012.01060.x
- Landreth, G. L. (2002). Play Therapy: The Art of the Relationship. Brunner-Routledge.
- Landreth, G. L. (2005). Child Parent Relationship Therapy (CPRT). Routledge.
- Lin, F., Zhou, Y., Du, Y., Qin, L., Zhao, Z., Xu, J., & Lei, H. (2012). Abnormal White Matter Integrity in Adolescents with Internet Addiction Disorder: A Tract-Based Spatial Statistics Study. PLoS ONE, 7(1), e30253. https://doi.org/10.1371/journal.pone.0030253
- Liu, J., Esmail, F., Li, L., Kou, Z., Li, W., Gao, X., Wang, Z., Tan, C., Zhang, Y., & Zhou, S. (2013). Decreased Frontal Lobe Function in People with Internet Addiction Disorder. Neural Regeneration Research, 8(32), 3225–3232. https://doi.org/10.3969/j.issn.1673-5374.2013.34.006
- National Center for Chronic Disease Prevention and Health Promotion (US) Office on Smoking and Health. (2012). Preventing Tobacco Use Among Youth and Young Adults: A Report of the Surgeon General. Centers for Disease Control and Prevention (US): https://www.ncbi.nlm.nih.gov/books/NBK99237/
- Palaus, M., Marron, E. M., Viejo-Sobera, R., & Redolar-Ripoll, D. (2017). Neural Basis of Video Gaming: A Systematic Review. Frontiers in Human Neuroscience, 11, 248. https://doi.org/10.3389/fnhum.2017.00248
- Peracchia, S., & Curcio, G. (2018). Exposure to Video Games: Effects on Sleep and on Post-Sleep Cognitive Abilities. A Systematic Review of Experimental Evidences. Sleep Science, 11(4), 302–314. https://doi.org/10.5935/1984-0063.20180046
- Rowan, C. (n.d.). The Impact of Technology on Child Sensory and Motor Development. http://www.sensoryprocessing.info/CrisRowan.pdf
- Yuan, K., Qin, W., Wang, G., Zeng, F., Zhao, L., Yang, X., Liu, P., Liu, J., Sun, J., von Deneen, K. M., Gong, Q., Liu, Y., & Tian, J. (2011). Microstructure Abnormalities in Adolescents with Internet Addiction Disorder. PLoS ONE, 6(6), e20708. https://doi.org/10.1371/journal.pone.0020708

ACKNOWLEDGMENTS

A huge thank you to the many people who have made this dream a reality:

To my team at Two Penny Publishing—Tom, Jodi, Sarah, Matt, and Adrian for your guidance and help.

To my graphic artist—Jeff for always over-delivering a fantastic final product.

To my family—Randy, Deb, Brandon, Gene, Audrey, and Marcia for loving me and helping to shape me into who I am.

To my friends, clients, and colleagues—for proofing, giving feedback, endorsing, and promoting. Specifically Kara Holt, Liana Lowenstein, Larry Rubin, Tara Moser, Phyllis Post, Sue Bratton, Jennifer Baggerly, Adam Alter, and Lynn Moran.

And, as always, to my husband Eric and son Kayne—for believing in me and giving me the opportunity to fulfill my dreams with your support. I love you so much.

Made in United States
Orlando, FL
05 December 2023